LES MISERABLES

NOTES

including
- *Life of Victor Hugo*
- *Hugo the Writer*
- *Synopsis*
- *Summaries and Commentaries*
- *Review Questions and Essay Topics*
- *Selected Bibliography*
- Les Miserables *Genealogy*

by
Amy L. Marsland, Ph.D.
Harpur College
State University of New York

and
George Klin
Dept. of Foreign Languages
Atlantic Community College

Cliffs® **Notes**
INCORPORATED
LINCOLN, NEBRASKA 68501

Editor

Gary Carey, M.A.
University of Colorado

Consulting Editor

James L. Roberts, Ph.D.
Department of English
University of Nebraska

ISBN 0-8220-0735-5
© Copyright 1968, 1993
by
Cliffs Notes, Inc.
All Rights Reserved
Printed in U.S.A.

2000 Printing

Cliffs Notes, Inc.   Lincoln, Nebraska

CONTENTS

Les Misérables Notes

LIFE OF VICTOR HUGO

Victor Hugo was born on February 26, 1802, the son of a Breton mother and a father from northeastern France. His works show the influence of both racial strains: the poetic mysticism which marks Celtic literature from the Arthurian romances to Chateaubriand and the earthy vigor of the peasant of Lorraine.

Although Hugo later claimed he descended from a family of the minor nobility, his father, General Joseph Léopold Hugo, was the son of a carpenter, and like many men of the Napoleonic era, he rose through valor and merit to power and influence in Napoleon's citizen army.

General Hugo was attached to the entourage of Joseph Bonaparte, and his duties took him to Naples and to Spain. Victor visited him in Italy at the age of five and went to school in Madrid in 1811. Traces of these exotic memories will be found in his later poetry and plays. However, Mme. Hugo, a strong-minded and independent personality, did not like the unstable existence of an army wife and in 1812 settled in Paris. Here her three sons, of whom Victor was the youngest, received their first orderly education.

As a result of this estrangement, General Hugo formed a liaison that took on a permanent character, and after Waterloo the Hugos arranged a separation. General Hugo, however, refused to leave his sons with their mother and sent them to a boarding school.

Victor Hugo suffered, but not acutely, from this separation from his mother. He was already, at fifteen, in love with a neighbor's daughter, Adèle Foucher, and was planning a brilliant literary career so that he could marry her. An excellent student in literature and mathematics, in 1817 he received an honorable mention from the Académie Française for a poem entered in a competition, and in 1819 he won first place in another national poetry contest.

When his mother died in 1821, he refused to accept any financial support from his father and endured a year of acute poverty, but in 1822 his first volume of verse, *Odes at Poésies diverses*, won him a pension of 1,000 francs a year from Louis XVIII. On the strength of this he promptly married Adèle, and during the following years four children were born to the Hugos.

Already in 1824 Hugo was a member of the group of Romantic rebels who were attempting to overthrow the domination of classical literature, and in 1830 he became one of the leaders when his historical drama *Hernani* won the theater audience and broke the stranglehold of the classical format on the stage. It also made him rich, and during the next 15 years six plays, four volumes of verse, and the novel *Notre Dame de Paris* (The Hunchback of Notre Dame) established his position as the leading writer of France.

His connection with the stage also had effects on his personal life. In 1831 a rupture developed in the Hugo household when Sainte-Beuve, one of Hugo's closest friends and a well known Romantic critic, fell in love with Adèle Hugo and received some encouragement. The next year Hugo met a young actress, Juliette Drouet, who in 1833 became his mistress and quit the stage. Supported by a modest pension from Hugo, she became for the next fifty years his unpaid secretary and traveling companion.

In 1843 the failure of Hugo's last drama, *Les Burgraves,* and the death of his eldest daughter, drowned on her honeymoon, caused him to abandon poetry temporarily for politics. This sharp change of direction in Hugo's career was paralleled in the lives of a number of other Romantic authors, for instance, Lamartine and George Sand. In the face of a rapidly growing and changing French society, plagued by social problems of all kinds, many writers came to feel that it was not enough simply to write beautiful and moving works of art but that their talents should be more directly applied in helping the poor and oppressed. In effect, this changing mood marks the end of the Romantic era in French literature and the opening of the Realistic-Naturalistic period.

Originally a royalist like his mother, Hugo's reconciliation with his father in 1822 broadened his political views and he was, by this time, a moderate republican. He was made a peer of France in 1845 and made a number of speeches on social questions of the time.

With the revolution of 1848 and the founding of the Second Republic, Hugo was elected deputy to the Constitutional Assembly. Three years later, when Louis Napoleon abolished the republic by a coup d'etat and reestablished the Empire, Hugo risked his life trying vainly to rally the workers of Paris against the new emperor and had to flee to Brussels disguised as a workman.

The next 19 years of Hugo's life were spent in exile, first on the island of Jersey, then on Guernsey. His family and Mlle. Drouet accompanied him into exile. From his island in the English channel Hugo continued to inveigh against the man he considered the perverter of republican liberties, and 1852 and 1853 saw the writing of the satires *Napoléon le Petit* and *Les Châtiments*. He also turned again to poetry and the novel, publishing the philosophical *Les Contemplations* and the remarkable "history of man's conscience," *La Légende des Siecles.* Three novels also occupied him: *Les Misérables,* first begun many years before; *Les Travailleurs de la Mer* (1866), and *L'Homme qui rit* (1869).

Following the Franco-Prussian War and the fall of the Empire in 1870-71, Hugo returned to Paris. It was a triumphal return: he was greeted at the station by an immense crowd and was accompanied through the streets to his hotel amid shouts of "Vive Victor Hugo!" He remained in Paris throughout the siege of the city, and the revenues from the first French publication of *Les Châtiments* bought two cannons to defend the city. In 1871 the death of one of his sons took him for some time to Brussels; he then returned to Guernsey until the death of another son brought him back to Paris in 1873. He was elected to the Senate in 1876, but two years later poor health forced him to return to the tranquility of Guernsey. His later years were saddened not only by the death of his sons but by that of Mme. Hugo in 1868 and of Mlle. Drouet in 1882.

Hugo himself died in 1885 at the age of eighty-three. His last wishes were, "I leave 50,000 francs to the poor. I wish to be taken to the cemetery in the hearse customarily used for the poor. I refuse the prayers of all churches. I believe in God."

Despite the austerity of his wishes, his funeral was the occasion of a national tribute to France's greatest writer. His body lay in state under the Arc de Triomphe guarded by horsemen with flaming torches, while twelve poets watched around his bier. On the day of the funeral, a million spectators followed his cortege, and the Pantheon, a church under Napoleon III, was once again transformed into a national sepulcher to receive his remains. He lies there today, amid France's great men.

Victor Hugo has frequently been criticized for vanity of character and shallowness of mind. The vanity of which he was accused is largely justified by the immense scope of his talents, unparalleled in literary history since Shakespeare and Goethe. It is true that he was not a profound thinker, but his devotion to "the good, the beautiful and the true," if uncritical, was instinctive and sincere. The people of France whom he loved have judged him better than the critics, and he remains to this day one of France's best-loved authors.

HUGO THE WRITER

Hugo's career, covering as it does most of the nineteenth century, spans both the Romantic and the Realist movements, but it cannot be said—despite Hugo's initial fame as a Romantic poet—to belong to one movement more than the other. His superb use of the colorful and significant detail, which produces exoticism in *Les Orientales* and local color in *Notre Dame de Paris*, becomes, when applied to the modern scene in *Les Misérables*, the sheerest realism. He is never, like Stendhal and Flaubert, objective and impassive in the face of the scene he describes, but he is always more interested in the external world than in the inner world of his own feelings; and the passionate spirit with which he describes what he sees is no more "romantic" than Zola's. If the themes of his poetry are often Romantic, his concern for art and technique makes him a brother to the Parnassians; and the epic quality of all his work links him with Chateaubriand and de Vigny, on the one hand, and with Zola, on the other. Only as a dramatist can he be considered purely a Romantic.

POETRY

Victor Hugo is among the greatest poets of a century of great poets. He claims this place not only because of the immense volume of his production, spread over nearly sixty years, but because of the variety of his themes and techniques.

Hugo's poems deal with an unusually wide range of themes. Romantic love and the evocation of nature are, of course, among them; but he also deals ably and movingly with current events of the day, descriptions of exotic and historic scenes, philosophy, parenthood and grandparenthood. His satires are as powerful as his lyrics; no strain is foreign to his lyre.

As a poetic technician, Hugo is a great innovator. He is one of the first to move away from the classical tradition of the Alexandrine couplet (which, nevertheless, he can handle magnificently) toward more complex and subtle forms of verse borrowed from the Middle Ages and from his own rich imagination. He reshapes not only the form, but the vocabulary of poetry, and injects it with a new variety and richness.

In contrast with most poets who are skilled in the use of only two or three poetic devices, Hugo is master of all. He is a splendid rhetorician but is also adept in the music of poetry. And he employs not only the music of skillful phrasing but the sound of the words themselves to awaken and charm the inner ear of the imagination. When in *L'Expiation* he writes "Après une plaine blanche, une autre plaine blanche," not only the repetitive phrase but the flat echo of the open vowels call up the image of Russia's endless expanses.

He is also a master of imagery, not only simile and metaphor, but symbol. He advises poets to interpret their "interior world of images, thoughts, sentiments, love and burning passion to fecundate this world" through "the other visible universe all around you" (*Pan*, 1831); and he can almost always find a vivid and exact natural parallel to the landscape of his soul. In all these respects, he is the precursor and inspiration for the poets who follow: Baudelaire, the Parnassians, and the Symbolists are all to a large extent his disciples and his debtors.

DRAMA

In the Preface to *Cromwell* of 1827-28, Hugo serves as spokesman for the Romantic movement in attacking classical drama and in laying down the precepts of the new drama to be. He condemns the rigidity of both classical format and language: the unities of time, scene, and action, and the false and formal elegance of speech. He calls for a richer and more flexible verse, which will more closely approximate the rhythm of everyday speech, and a more flexible format, which will allow comedy and tragedy to mingle in Shakespearean fashion, just as they do in life itself. Weary of the eternal Greek kings and Roman heroes of the classical stage, he suggests that more recent history may also provide suitable themes for drama and that a bourgeois or a bandit may also sometimes possess enough nobility to transform a stage.

These precepts he exemplified in his own plays, some of which are in prose as well as in verse and which generally deal with some dramatic episode from European history. The subjects of *Marie Tudor* and *Lucrezia Borgia* are self-explanatory. *Hernani*—which quite literally caused a riot at its first performance—sets at odds a noble Spanish bandit and Charles V, Emperor of Spain; in *Ruy Blas* a valet, through the love of a queen, temporarily becomes head of state.

We cannot today appreciate Hugo's plays as wholeheartedly as did his contemporaries. His plots with their disguises and recognitions seem a little too melodramatic; his daring adventurers and his perfect, passionate, unattainable heroines are two-dimensional. Nevertheless, particularly in their historical accuracy of incident and decor, they represent a great stride toward realism in the drama; and in the stage's own terms, some of them are still "marvelous theater."

THE NOVEL

Hugo wrote several novels, but the only three that have continued to be much read today are *Les Misérables; Notre Dame de Paris;* and *Les Travailleurs de la Mer,* the story of a young fisherman who fights the sea to salvage a wreck and win the girl he loves but who gives her up when he learns she prefers another man.

Les Travailleurs de la Mer is read chiefly for its magnificent evocations of the sea, but *Notre Dame de Paris* is known the world over. Set in medieval Paris, it is one of those Romantic historical novels inspired by Sir Walter Scott, and on more than one score it bears comparison with *Ivanhoe*. Both are popular classics; both have suspenseful and melodramatic plots; and both contain character sketches which, despite their lack of depth, have remained vivid and memorable for a century. Just as every English school child knows Rowena, Rebecca, Ivanhoe, and Sir Brian de Bois Guilbert, so every French reader knows the poor but beautiful gypsy Esmeralda with her little goat; the alchemist-priest Claude Frollo, who desires her; and Quasimodo, the "hunchback of Notre Dame," who loves her and tries to save her.

The chief fascination of *Notre Dame de Paris*, however, lies in its powerful and living recreation of the Middle Ages. Hugo consulted many historical archives and accounts in his research for the novel, but the scenes of Paris life seem the work not of a scholar but of an eyewitness.

Les Misérables has many of the same qualities as *Notre Dame de Paris*, but it is a far more complex creation. As early as 1829 Hugo began to gather notes for a book that would tell the story of "a saint, a man, a woman, and a child," but over the years it became enriched by a throng of new characters and multiple accretions from Hugo's philosophy and experience. When it was finally published in 1862 it had attained, both in quality and quantity, an epic sweep.

In both thought and feeling, *Les Misérables* is far more profound than *Notre Dame de Paris*. In writing it, Hugo came to grips with the social problems of his own day; and this demanded much reflection upon the nature of society and, therefore, upon the nature of man. In 1830, the average life expectancy of a French worker's child was two years. Hugo, unlike many of his contemporaries, did not consider this statistic as "inevitable," or "the fault of the parents," but evaluated it in human terms, and cried out that suffering of such magnitude was intolerable and that such conditions must be changed through social action. What social action he considered desirable he shows us indirectly by portraying children who need to be fed, men who need jobs, and women who need protection; but also directly through M. Madeleine, who serves as an example of the ideal employer, and through the students of the 1832 revolt who demand legislation that will make possible equal education, equal opportunity, and genuine brotherhood among men.

But to support this social action Hugo must be convinced, and convince others, that the poor, the outcast — the *misérables* — are worth saving: that even the most impudent, scruffy street gamin has something to contribute to society, that even the most hardened convict is capable of great good. And the most appealing and enduring quality of *Les Misérables* is the fact that it is permeated by this unquenchable belief in the spiritual possibilities of man.

Plot and Structure

Like that of *Notre Dame de Paris*, the plot of *Les Misérables* is fundamentally melodramatic; its events are often improbable and it moves in the realm of the socially and psychologically abnormal. But this melodrama is deliberate; Hugo has chosen an extreme example, the conversion of a convict into a saint, to illustrate a general truth: that man is perfectible.

Moreover, within this general framework, the sequence and inter-relation of the events are credible, and the structure is very carefully plotted. Like a good play, it opens on a situation of high suspense, rises to two increasingly tense climaxes at the ends of Part Three and Part Four, and arrives at a satisfactory and logical denouement in Part Five. Its two themes, the struggle between good and evil in the soul of one man and society's struggle toward a greater good, are skillfully interwoven, and Hugo effectively immortalizes this struggle in our imaginations by a number of striking visual tableaux.

Character

Psychological subtleties are not Hugo's forte. He does not, probably cannot, delve into the baffling paradoxes, the complexities, the idiosyncracies of the soul. His gift is for the fundamental truth. Valjean is a simple character dominated by one powerful emotion: *caritas* (char-ity—active, outgoing love for others). He helps a prostitute, protects his workers, gives constantly to the poor. His very *raison d'être* is liter-ally love, since his existence revolves around Cosette and when she leaves him he dies.

Javert is the watchdog of the social order. Marius is the incarnation of the romantic lover. Enjolras is the incorruptible revolutionary. All of Hugo's characters can be briefly described—in other words, labeled.

But this simplicity has its own value. It allows the writer to analyze in depth a particular emotion, like a scientist studying an isolated germ. No one has captured better than Victor Hugo the arduous path of virtue or the poignancy of love. Valjean's deathbed scene has brought tears to the most sophisticated reader.

Of course, Hugo's truth is the poet's not the psychologist's. He takes great liberties with reality. His characters do not always evolve in con-vincing steps. Valjean's conversion is almost miraculous, Thénardier's degradation unmotivated. They are larger than life. Marius loves pas-sionately, Valjean is a modern saint, Thénardier a Satanic villain.

But these are superficial criticisms. Hugo only distorts details: he scrupulously respects the basic integrity of the character. *Les Misérables* is the archetypal representation of eternal human emotions such as love, hate, and abnegation.

Style

Style is the reflection of the man and it is therefore not surprising that a writer of Victor Hugo's enormous vitality should abandon classical restraint. Hugo revels in language. Ideas are stated and restated. Places are exhaustively described. Characters do not speak, they harangue, lament, eulogize. No doubt, Hugo's exuberance is excessive. His antitheses occasionally grow tiresome. His discourse can degenerate into verbiage. His pronouncements sometimes sound hollow, or worse, false. But the defect is minor, for Hugo suffers only from an overabundance of riches. His style is a mighty organ.

He is at home in every idiom from the argot of the underworld to the intellectual tone of student discussion. He captures the slangy sarcasm of the gamin, the eloquence of the idealist, the lyricism of the lover. His expository prose, fed by an insatiable curiosity, deals with a range of subjects rarely encountered in a novel. Hugo writes with an absolute command of the *mot juste*, about history, logistics, philosophy, religion. and political morality.

He remains, of course, the greatest word painter in the French language. In *Les Misérables* no less than in his poetry, he justifies his claim of being "the sonorous echo of the universe." Countless vignettes and a few bravura pieces such as the description of the Battle of Waterloo invest his novels with a heightened sense of reality. Few writers can rival the vividness and eloquence of Hugo's style.

SYNOPSIS

Jean Valjean, after spending 19 years in jail and in the galleys for stealing a loaf of bread and for several attempts to escape, is finally released. But his past keeps haunting him. At Digne he is repeatedly refused shelter for the night. Only the saintly bishop, Monseigneur Myriel, welcomes him. Valjean repays his host's hospitality by stealing his silverware. When the police bring him back, the bishop protects his errant guest by pretending that the silverware is a gift. With a pious lie, he convinces them that the convict has promised to reform. After one more theft, Jean Valjean does indeed repent. Under the name of M. Madeleine he starts a factory and brings prosperity to the town of Montreuil.

Next, Hugo introduces the pathetic young girl Fantine. Alone and burdened with an illegitimate child, she is on the way back to her home town of Montreuil, to find a job. On the road she entrusts her daughter to an innkeeper and his wife, the Thénardiers.

In Montreuil, Fantine finds a job in Madeleine's factory and attains a modicum of prosperity. Unfortunately she is fired and, at the same time, must meet increasing financial demands by the Thénardiers. Defeated by her difficulties, Fantine turns to prostitution. Tormented by a local idler, she causes a disturbance and is arrested by Inspector Javert. Only Madeleine's forceful intervention keeps her out of jail. She catches a fever, however, and her health deteriorates dangerously. Death is imminent and M. Madeleine promises to bring her daughter, Cosette, to her.

Madeleine, however, is faced with serious problems. A man has been arrested as Jean Valjean and is about to be condemned for his crimes. After a night of agonizing moral conflict, Madeleine decides to confess his past. At Arras, the seat of the trial, he dramatically exonerates the accused. A few days later he is arrested by Javert at Fantine's bedside. The shocking scene kills the young woman.

That same night Valjean escapes, but he is quickly recaptured and sent to Toulon, a military port. One day he saves a sailor about to fall from the rigging. He plunges into the sea and manages to escape by establishing the belief that he has drowned. He uses his precarious freedom to go to Montfermeil, the location of the Thénardiers' inn. After burying his money in the woods, he frees Cosette from the Thénardiers' abominable guardianship and takes her into the protective anonymity of Paris.

In Paris he lives like a recluse in a dilapidated tenement, the Gorbeau House, in an outlying district. In spite of his precautions, however, Javert manages to track him down. Valjean is forced to flee abruptly. After a hectic chase and imminent capture he finds a miraculous refuge in a convent. With the cooperation of the gardener, Fauchelevent, a man whose life he has saved in the past, Valjean persuades the prioress to take him on as assistant gardener and to enroll Cosette as a pupil. Valjean and Cosette spend several happy years in the isolation of the convent.

Hugo now turns to another leading character, Marius. Marius is a seventeen-year-old who lives with his grandfather, M. Gillenormand, a relic of the Old Regime. In a nearby town Georges Pontmercy, Marius' father, a hero of the Napoleonic wars, lives in retirement. M. Gillenormand, by threatening to disinherit Marius, has forced Georges Pontmercy to relinquish custody of his son. He has completed the estrangement by communicating his aversion for Pontmercy to Marius. Consequently, the young man reacts almost impassively to his father's death. A fortuitous conversation reveals to Marius the depths of his father's love for him and, indignant at his grandfather's deception, he leaves home.

He takes refuge in the Latin Quarter and falls in with a group of radical students, the Friends of the A.B.C. Marius, who under his father's posthumous influence has just switched his allegiance from the monarchy to Napoleon, falls into a state of intellectual bewilderment. Material difficulties increase his unhappiness. Finally he manages to create a tolerable existence by finding a modest job, living frugally, and withdrawing into his inner dreams.

His peace is shattered when he falls passionately in love with a beautiful young girl in the Luxembourg Gardens. She is Jean Valjean's ward, Cosette. Too timid for bold actions, he courts her silently. A fatal indiscretion ruins his nascent love affair. He quizzes the doorman where the girl lives and a week later she moves without leaving an address. For a long time Marius is unable to find a clue to his sweetheart's whereabouts and is overcome by despair.

Coincidence puts him back on the track. One day curiosity impels him to observe his neighbors through a hole in the wall. He glimpses a family—father, mother, and two daughters—living in unspeakable squalor. Soon after he witnesses the entrance of a philanthropist, M. Leblanc, and his daughter. To his immense surprise, the daughter is Cosette. His jubilation is replaced by consternation when he discovers that his neighbors are planning to draw M. Leblanc into a trap the same evening. Marius contacts the police and on the instructions of Inspector Javert returns to his room.

When Leblanc comes back, Marius' neighbor identifies himself as Thénardier, ties up his victim, and demands an exorbitant ransom. The plot fails with the timely arrival of the inspector. In the confusion of the arrest Leblanc escapes.

Once again, the young girl has vanished. But Thénardier's daughter, who is selflessly in love with Marius, manages to find his sweetheart for him.

After worshiping Cosette from afar, Marius summons the courage to declare his love. Cosette reciprocates. For a whole month the couple lives a chaste and secret idyll, secret because Cosette intuitively guesses Valjean's hostility to the man who is usurping his place.

Marius' happiness is unwittingly shattered by Valjean who, disturbed by a secret warning and the growing popular unrest in Paris, has decided to take Cosette to England. As a first step he moves to a hideaway prepared for this kind of emergency.

Absorbed by his love, Marius has been unaware of the deteriorating political situation. Now his private crisis is echoed by the crisis of an imminent insurrection. His friend Enjolras directs the erection of a barricade in front of the Corinth wine shop. The first enemy he has to deal with is found within the rebels' ranks. It is Javert, who is unmasked as a spy and tied up to await execution.

Marius, driven by despair, decides to seek death in the insurrection. He joins the fighters at the barricade and fights valiantly to the end. Valjean also joins the insurgents, but for special reasons. He has discovered Marius' relationship with Cosette and his role in the revolution. For Cosette's sake he decides to protect the life of the man he abhors.

Before the final assault, Valjean volunteers to execute Javert. Instead he spares the inspector's life and sends him away. Then Valjean returns to the barricade as the few surviving defenders are driven inside the wine shop. He seizes the seriously wounded Marius, disappears into a manhole, and undertakes a heroic and harrowing passage through the sewers of Paris. Unfortunately, Javert arrests him at the exit. However, he allows Valjean to take Marius to his grandfather and later, in a quandary, he releases Valjean. But he cannot forgive himself for this breach of duty and commits suicide.

Marius' life has a happier epilog. He recuperates from his wounds and overcomes his grandfather's hostility to his marriage. The marriage, however, is a mortal blow to Valjean. He has confessed his past to Marius, and the latter, in spite of his magnanimity, slowly estranges Cosette from Valjean. Marius does not know that Valjean is the man who saved his life in the sewers. Without Cosette, Valjean's life loses its meaning and he slowly withers away. Thénardier, however, unwittingly reveals to Marius that Valjean is his savior, and Marius and Cosette arrive in time to console Jean Valjean on his deathbed.

LIST OF CHARACTERS

Monseigneur Charles François-Bienvenu Myriel

Saintly bishop whose compassionate treatment causes the reformation of the ex-convict Valjean. He is also called "M. Bienvenu."

Mlle. Baptistine

Sister of the bishop.

Mme. Magliore

Housekeeper for the bishop and his sister.

Jean Valjean

Ex-convict still pursued by the law, who strives for moral perfection and achieves a kind of sainthood in his love for the little orphan Cosette. He is also known as M. Madeleine and M. Leblanc.

Little Gervais

Chimney sweep from whom Valjean steals a coin, his last criminal act for which Javert inexorably trails him.

Fantine

A beautiful waif of unknown parentage who comes to Paris at the age of fifteen. She falls in love with Tholomyès and bears an illegitimate child, Cosette. Forced to give up her child, Fantine is crushed and ultimately destroyed by adversity.

Cosette

Illegitimate daughter of Fantine, originally named Euphrasie. She has a wretched childhood as the ward of the brutal innkeeper Thénardier, but later finds happiness in Valjean's devoted care and in the love of a young man.

Félix Tholomyès

A student, Fantine's lover and father of Cosette.

Thénardier

An evil innkeeper who mistreats Cosette during her childhood, lures Valjean into an ambush, and commits various other crimes. He is also known as Jondrette and Fabantou.

Mme. Thénardier

A virago whose sweeping malevolence spares only her husband and her two daughters.

Eponine

Older daughter of the Thénardiers. As a child she is spoiled at Cosette's expense; later she becomes a ragged, hungry adolescent. Her love for Marius first endangers, then saves his life.

Azelma

Second daughter of the Thénardiers. Spoiled at first, her life becomes as miserable as her sister's.

Gavroche

The Thénardiers' oldest son, a typical Paris gamin. He dies heroically at the barricades in the revolution of 1832.

Two little boys

The Thénardiers' youngest children. Given by their parents to an acquaintance, Magnon, they wander the streets of Paris after she is arrested. Gavroche's protection gives them temporary solace.

Inspector Javert

An incorruptible policeman. He makes it his life's work to track down Jean Valjean.

Fauchelevent

Valjean, as Madeleine, saves his life; Fauchelevent later is gardener at the convent of the Little Picpus and gives shelter to Valjean and Cosette.

Bamatabois

An idler of the town who torments Fantine by putting snow down her back.

Champmathieu

The man accused of being Jean Valjean, on whose behalf "Madeleine" reveals his true identity.

Sister Simplicity

A nun who lies to save Valjean from Javert.

Boulatruelle

An old roadworker, ex-convict, and minor associate of the underworld chiefs. He is constantly seeking buried treasure in the forest near Montfermeil.

The Prioress

Head of the convent where Valjean and Cosette live for several years.

Mestienne and Gribier

The two gravediggers. Mestienne, friend of Fauchelevent, dies suddenly, and his place is taken by Gribier, nearly causing Valjean to be buried alive.

M. Gillenormand

Relic of the Enlightenment, he is hostile to the romantic love and liberal politics of his grandson Marius.

Mlle. Gillenormand

Gillenormand's daughter, a lackluster old maid whose interests are limited to devotional practices.

Marius Pontmercy

An idealistic student who falls passionately in love with Cosette and later marries her.

Colonel Georges Pontmercy

Marius' father, an officer of Napoleon's, named by him a colonel, a baron, and an officer of the Legion of Honor.

Lieutenant Théodule Gillenormand

M. Gillenormand's grandnephew. He is asked to spy on his cousin Marius.

Magnon

Friend of Mme. Thénardier. She bears two illegitimate boys, for whom M. Gillenormand, her former employer, pays all expenses. When the boys die, the Thénardiers gladly give her their two youngest sons in exchange for a share of the money.

M. Mabeuf

An old horticulturist and bibliophile, now a churchwarden. He is instrumental in revealing to Marius the truth about his father. Later, driven by destitution, he dies a heroic death at the barricades.

Mother Plutarch

Servant of M. Mabeuf; shares his poverty to the end.

Montparnasse
Claquesous
Gueulemer
Babet

The four chiefs of the Paris underworld, occasionally associated with Thénardier.

Enjolras

An uncompromising political radical who dies courageously as the leader of a group of student insurrectionists.

Grantaire

Enjolras' friend. He is a drunken cynic who redeems a useless existence by sharing Enjolras' death before a firing squad.

Combeferre

Friend of Enjolras and second in command of the student insurrectionists.

Courfeyrac

A student. With Enjolras and Combeferre, he helps incite and lead the insurrection.

Jean Prouvaire

A friend of Enjolras and one of the group of revolutionaries. He is rich, sensitive, and intelligent.

Bahoral

A law student and revolutionary. He is good-humored and capricious, and refuses to be serious in his studies.

Joly

A student. A hypochondriac, he is nevertheless a gay and happy companion.

Bossuet

A student revolutionary. Although he signs his name "Lègle (de Meaux)," he is called Bossuet (Bald), Laigle (The Eagle), and occasionally Lesgle.

Feuilly

A self-taught worker, and an ardent insurrectionist.

Le Cabuc

Shoots a porter during the insurrection and is executed by Enjolras. May actually have been Claquesous.

SUMMARIES AND COMMENTARIES

PART ONE: FANTINE

Book I

Summary

In 1815, M. Charles François-Bienvenu Myriel has been Bishop of Digne for nine years. He is seventy-five years old and lives only with a sister Baptistine, ten years younger than he, and an old servant, Madame Magloire, the same age as his sister.

The bishop's background destined him to a worldly career. His father was a counselor at the Parlement of Aix and was grooming his son to be his successor. The young man married at eighteen and cut an impressive figure in society. But the Revolution changed his destiny. Exile, his wife's death, the destruction of the ancient order, perhaps some private grief, turned M. Myriel toward the priesthood.

M. Myriel became a priest of ineffable goodness. His appointment as bishop by Napoleon was a blessing to his diocese. He turned over his vast and sumptuous palace to the sick and converted the hospital into his own Spartan residence. The only luxury that he has retained from a more comfortable past are a few silver pieces: six knives and forks, a soup ladle, and two candlesticks.

Not only the resources of the church, but most of his own, are used for the benefit of the indigent. Out of a salary of 15,000 francs, 14,000 are earmarked for charity. For the sake of the poor the bishop willingly hazards his reputation. He requests funds for the maintenance of a carriage, risking criticism for this extravagance, in order to give the money to orphans and foundlings. His sacrifice does not prevent him from visiting his flock on foot, by donkey, or by some other modest means of transportation. Tirelessly he ministers to the sick, consoles the dying, and preaches the moral life. He does not demand the impossible and never condemns hastily. His front door is always unlocked, a perpetual invitation for those in need.

Only a few events interrupt his saintly daily routine. On one occasion, he consoles a convict during his last night on earth and attends his execution. The experience leaves him with a lingering impression of horror and doubts about the social order.

The bishop's pastoral duties involve him in another experience that illustrates his unflinching zeal. Eager to visit an isolated parish village, he ventures alone into the mountains where the bandit Cravatte has his hideout. At the village, he wants to sing a Te Deum but finds the parish too poor to provide the necessary episcopal ornaments for the service. Help comes from an unexpected source: the thief Cravatte sends him a trunk filled with the treasures he has stolen from another church, Notre Dame of Embrun. The bishop uses them for his service, but we are left in suspense as to whether he then returns them to Embrun or sells them and gives the funds to the hospital.

Humble with the underprivileged, M. Bienvenu (as his parishioners call him because of his kindness to them) can be cutting with the complacently wealthy. He refutes the amoral materialism of a senator with a sarcastic sermon, an ironic compliment.

His irony is reserved exclusively for the selfish, however, and he treats honorable opponents with consideration and courtesy. When he hears of the serious illness of G., a member of the Convention of 1793 that sent so many to the guillotine, he feels compelled to pay him a pastoral visit, and in a long conversation marked by mutual respect the two argue the value of the Revolution. With uncommon understanding, the bishop acknowledges its merits and, in a reversal of roles, concludes by asking the conventionist's blessing.

Commentary

It is often the case that the opening lines of a book set the keynote for the whole. Here, it is the Bishop of Digne who sets the spiritual keynote for *Les Misérables*.

A truly good man or woman is one of the most difficult characters for a writer to portray convincingly. Notice that in describing the bishop, Hugo does not simply tell us "This man is a saint." Instead, he introduces him to us gradually and lets us form our own conclusions. We learn first what people say about his past. Then we see him in action, giving away his palace and his income; and we hear him speak — simply and wisely to his parishioners, gaily to his sister, wittily to the great. In Chapters 5-9 we penetrate further into his private life and learn that he lives as unpretentiously in his bedroom as he does in public, and that his sister and servant love and revere him even more than his parishioners. To add more conviction still to this straightforward account. Hugo lets us read at firsthand the bishop's personal budget and his sister's letter to an old friend, and subjects him to two difficult tests: a test of courage with Cravatte, the thief, a test of charity with G., the conventionist. And when, finally, we are given a glimpse of his inner thoughts we are not surprised at the radiance we find there.

Most of all, however, it is the touch of humor—even of the sardonic —which Hugo gives M. Myriel that makes him believable. The bishop is not above a bit of larceny in a good cause, nor is he free from personal and class prejudice. But he is constantly being changed by what he believes; his inner light changes his own personality as well as that of those around him.

The bishop is also important to Hugo as a social symbol. A man of the Old Regime, he has accepted his loss of privilege without bitterness, and though a student of the divine, he is not blind to the flaws in human law. In his sympathetic treatment of both the bishop and the conventionist G., and in showing that a reconciliation between them is possible, Hugo is indirectly urging his readers to put progress above party and to unite to lift from the poor the terrible burden that, more than 80 years after the Revolution, they are still suffering.

Book II

Summary

At the beginning of October, 1815, a disreputable-looking traveler enters Digne on foot. In spite of his money, he is repeatedly refused food and shelter for the night with harsh words and threats. A fierce hound routs him from a doghouse when he mistakes it for a worker's hut. Despairingly he sums up his plight with the pathetic cry, "I am not even a dog!"

On the advice of a kindly passerby he tries the door of Monseigneur Myriel. He bluntly introduces himself as Jean Valjean, an ex-convict recently released from prison. To his surprise the bishop welcomes him warmly, inviting him to share his supper, giving him advice, and finally offering him a bed for the night. Even more remarkable, he treats Valjean with unfailing courtesy and ignores the stigma of his past.

Valjean's past is a tragic story. Originally a primitive but uncorrupted creature, when he was twenty-six years old he was condemned to a five-year jail term for stealing a loaf of bread to feed his widowed sister and her large family. Repeated attempts to escape lengthened his sentence to 19 years. In jail, the merciless treatment he endured corrupted his fundamental potentialities for good into an implacable hatred for society. The continuous hostility he has encountered since his release has only confirmed this hatred.

The bishop's kindness moves Valjean profoundly but does not regenerate him. Rising stealthily in the middle of the night, the ex-convict steals his host's silver from a cupboard above the sleeping man's head — indeed, he is prepared to kill the bishop if he wakes. The police, however, catch him when he is making his escape and bring him back to the bishop. This time his crime will bring him life imprisonment. However, Monseigneur Myriel pretends that the silverware is a legitimate gift and in a gesture of supreme kindness, even adds his candlesticks to it — the only objects of value he has left. As Jean Valjean is leaving he exacts his reward, "Don't forget," he tells the astonished man, "that you promised me to use this silver to become an honest man."

Still Jean Valjean's conversion is not complete. On a deserted road, he steals a coin from an itinerant chimney sweep, Little Gervais. But this last contemptible act sickens him of himself, and in a paroxysm of remorse he resolves to amend his life.

Commentary

When we first meet Jean Valjean, he is in fact less than a dog. A dog may be a useful animal; Jean Valjean is a dangerous one. Even before he went to the galleys he was more animal than man, moved only by an instinctive loyalty to those of his own litter, as brutishly ignorant of evil as of good. For Hugo, the fact that Valjean has educated himself in prison is promising; at the moment, however, education has only served to make him vicious.

The penal laws of the nineteenth century seem absurd to us, but they stem from the primitive mores of tribal society when most property is held in common and theft is a crime often punishable by death. Under the influence of utilitarian philosophy, which considered environment rather than original sin to be the most important element in character formation, thinking men in the eighteenth and nineteenth centuries began to take a new look at the legal system, and to call for milder laws and a prison system which would rehabilitate rather than degrade the offender. Hugo shares these enlightened views, and in fact his desire for reform of the penal system was the original inspiration for *Les Misérables*.

Impressive is the skill with which Hugo uses an external visual impression to evoke an internal conflict. Hugo was artist as well as writer, and in the scene in the bishop's room he gives us no sound, almost no motion. What we see, what we remember, is a darkness in which a threatening weapon hangs, the gleaming oval of the bishop's face, and between the two, the glimmer on the arms of the crucifix—an unforgettable pattern of black and white which symbolizes the unending conflict between good and evil, within and without, in man and in history.

The episode of the bishop's candlesticks is justly famous. The situation is dramatic, the psychology profound, and the artistry superb. Giving us only glimpses into the chaos in Jean Valjean's mind, Hugo deliberately awakens empathy by forcing us to provide our own explanations for Valjean's previous urge to murder, his theft, and his headlong flight.

Jean Valjean's conversion is completely convincing. He believes a totally hostile world surrounds him; the bishop has shown him good in it; but before he can change, he must see the evil in himself. Confronted by Little Gervais, he reacts with automatic cruelty—and then realizes that what the world has done to him he has done to someone even more defenseless. If he continues as he is, he will become one of those he hates; he has no choice but to change.

Book III

Summary

In this book we are introduced to one of the most pathetic characters in the novel, Fantine. A young girl of humble origins, she has retained her candor and compassion in the libertine company she keeps. Although she has taken a lover, Félix Tholomyès, she treats her affair with the romantic intensity of a first love. One summer day of the year 1817, Tholomyès arranges an outing in the country for Fantine and three more lighthearted couples. The day is spent in carefree amusements and concludes with a dinner in a restaurant, accompanied by banter and laughter.

But the festivities are marred by a macabre incident. An old horse dies before the eyes of the students and their girls. For Tholomyès it is only an occasion for a pun, but Fantine is touched by the nag's death.

The event seems to be the knell of her happiness. The men steal away from the restaurant and leave behind only a callous goodbye note — they are deserting their mistresses. Fantine's life is shattered, for she has had a little girl, Cosette, by Tholomyès and he has left her without resources.

Commentary

Victor Hugo was one of the earliest supporters in France of the "Shakespearean" approach to drama: mingling comedy with tragedy, and the sublime with the grotesque, to create a powerful contrast. Here, following the shadows and sufferings of Jean Valjean in Book II, he introduces youth, gaiety, and spring in the persons of Fantine and her companions on their student frolic; the effect of each tableau is heightened by the other.

However, the contrast is only apparent. In fact, we are about to begin another cycle of descent, despair, and regeneration, and as Jean Valjean plays out for us the fate of Man, Fantine and her baby will trace the fate of Woman and Child as they descend into the dark world of "les misérables."

In the earlier part of the nineteenth century, Balzac and the historical novelists developed the technique of the "significant detail," precise external description which nevertheless gives many clues to the inner nature of the person being described. We are so accustomed to this technique today that we automatically fill in any suggestive gaps in the text and find a writer like Hugo — who gives us the significant detail (Fantine's modest yet charming openwork blouse contrasted with the low necks of the other girls) but then goes on to explain its inner meaning (the purity and idealism of Fantine's passion contrasted with theirs) — old fashioned and boring. However it must be remembered that Hugo was not writing for college students or for a literary coterie; he wanted to reach the masses and was willing to say the same things in as many different ways as necessary to carry his message home, regardless of the esthetic effect. Hugo, in fact, was always willing to sacrifice his art to his conscience.

Book IV

Summary

In her distress, Fantine decides to return to her home town, Montreuil, taking with her her little girl, who is now two or three years old. On her way she becomes acquainted with Mme. Thénardier, an innkeeper's wife who is watching her two little daughters play at her doorstep. Misled by Mme. Thénardier's obvious affection for her children and unwilling to expose herself and Cosette to the shame that will result if she returns home an unmarried mother, Fantine entrusts her daughter to Mme. Thénardier.

It is an unfortunate decision. Mme. Thénardier is a vile and brutal creature whose affections are limited to her husband and her two daughters. Her husband is even worse than she. For him Cosette is nothing but an object for exploitation. He makes increasingly difficult financial demands on her mother and treats the child like a servant. Ill-fed, cold, and ragged, she becomes ugly and hostile.

Commentary

Artistic unity is complete in the confrontation of Fantine and Mme. Thénardier. The scene is a halfway house on Fantine's road to Montreuil; but she herself is at a halfway house, half Virgin with Child, half unmarried mother, on her road to Calvary. Mme. Thénardier too is at a halfway house, still capable of tenderness in the romantic dreams of her youth and in her love for her children, but under her husband's influence she has begun to lapse into brutality. Fantine's love for Cosette will save the child, but Cosette is also the agent who will bring about Mme. Thénardier's spiritual doom. Provided with a helpless victim, the innkeeper's wife will give way to all her worst instincts, and Cosette will totally corrupt her.

Book V, Chapters 1-7

Summary

In 1818 Montreuil becomes much more prosperous than it has previously been, thanks to a mysterious stranger, M. Madeleine, who has established a flourishing industry which he runs not only efficiently but with much humanity. He has become a father to his workers and to the whole community. His unfailing generosity has won him the post of mayor.

In 1821 a shadow is cast on M. Madeleine's good fortune. The local paper carries the announcement of M. Myriel's death. The next day, Madeleine appears dressed in black with a mourning band in his hat.

Somewhat later, M. Madeleine endears himself further to the town by a heroic exploit. As he walks down the street he sees one of his few enemies, Father Fauchelevent, caught under the wheels of his own cart. Immediate action is imperative. Madeleine offers a generous reward to induce the bystanders to lift the carriage, but the task requires Herculean strength and no one will volunteer. Faced by Fauchelevent's iminent death, Madeleine reluctantly undertakes the rescue himself and in one supreme effort manages to lift the carriage sufficiently to free the victim.

Paradoxically, Madeleine's heroism is to have ominous results for himself. It awakens the suspicions of his chief of police, Inspector Javert, for Madeleine's strength reminds him of Jean Valjean, an ex-convict he had known in Toulon.

This Javert is described at some length by Hugo. He is the epitome of the devoted police officer, incorruptible and relentless. He renders blind obedience to all constituted authority, and by the same token, condemns any and all lawbreakers to legal damnation.

Commentary

The transformation of Jean Valjean into M. Madeleine is improbable, coincidental, and comes out of the same formula box as The *Count of Monte Cristo;* nevertheless it is psychologically and artistically satisfying. We recognize, as Hugo does, that it is not enough for Jean Valjean to have experienced a spiritual conversion; this conversion must be tested in action; and the wider the field of action, the more satisfactory the test.

In any case, Hugo makes it clear that this transformation is not intended to be a happy ending. Jean Valjean is still in jeopardy, still, like Fantine, at a halfway house, as is shown by the presence of Javert.

Once every few hundred years, an author manages to delineate a character at once so individual and so universal that he becomes a new archetype in literature. Chaucer developed Pandarus; Victor Hugo created Javert. With consummate artistry Hugo blends Javert's history, his external appearance, and his inner nature to paint for us an unforgettable and terrifying portrait of a man-bloodhound, an inexorable and incorruptible police agent — a contradiction in terms in those days, when police forces were largely made up of "mouchards," or informers themselves involved in the criminal world.

What is most terrifying about Javert, however, is neither his persistence nor his purity but the fact that like a robot he decides always according to the letter of the law and not its spirit. Because of this, he makes both Fantine and Jean Valjean suffer acutely, but in the long run their weakness proves spiritual strength, and Javert's strength a spiritual weakness.

Book V, Chapters 8-13

Summary

Fantine has readily found a job in M. Madeleine's factory. Unaware of her child's plight, she feels a momentary surge of optimism as her fortune improves. Even though she is not very skillful, she earns enough to make ends meet. She rents a little room and furnishes it on credit. But clouds gather quickly on her peaceful horizon. Her letters to the Thénardiers arouse the curiosity of the town's busybodies. A certain Mme. Victurnien, a woman of malevolent piety, undertakes to investigate the mystery and discovers Fantine's secret.

Unbeknown to Madeleine, Fantine is abruptly fired by his assistant as "immoral." Unable to leave town because of her debts, she works at home, sewing coarse shirts for the soldiers of the garrison. Her ill-paid occupation earns her 12 sous a day and her daughter's board costs 10. Fantine works interminable hours and economizes desperately. In addition she suffers the opprobrium of the whole town. At first she cannot face the accusing fingers. Soon, however, she adopts a defiant attitude that rapidly becomes brazen.

Her situation grows worse. Overwork undermines her health. She is racked by a dry cough and contracts a fever. Her debts accumulate and the Thénardiers hound her unmercifully. One day they send her a frightful letter. Cosette needs a new wool skirt for the winter. It costs at least 10 francs. That night Fantine goes to the barber and sells him her hair for 10 francs and spends it on a skirt. Her mutilation causes her joy rather than regret. "My child is not cold any more," she thinks, "I dressed her with my hair." Unfortunately her sacrifice does Cosette no good. The Thénardiers have invented the story of the skirt to extort more money from her. Furious at having been unwittingly outsmarted, they give the skirt to their daughter Eponine and Cosette continues to shiver in the cold.

Misfortune also begins to take a moral toll. Fantine mistakenly attributes her troubles to Madeleine and begins to hate him. She has a sordid affair with a beggarly musician who beats her and then abandons her.

One day a new blow increases her misery. The insatiable Thénardiers bill her for 40 francs to cure a fever Cosette has supposedly contracted. Fantine tries to ignore their exorbitant demand, but not for long. One day Marguerite, Fantine's neighbor, finds her sitting on her bed overwhelmed by grief. When the candle suddenly lights Fantine's face, it reveals a gaping hole where her two front teeth had been. The desperate mother has sold them.

Fate now persecutes her relentlessly. She is reduced to the bare necessities of existence. Exhausted, she surrenders to dirt and rags. Creditors plague her. Bad health and endless work sap her vitality. Competition from cheap prison labor reduces her income to a pittance. The crushing blow comes from the Thénardiers. Now they want 100 francs and Fantine becomes a prostitute. But this is not the last ignominy. She is destined to drink her cup of pain to the dregs.

In January, 1823, a certain Bamatabois, one of the local idlers, amuses himself by insulting a wretched creature soliciting on the street. Exasperated by her indifference, he sadistically pushes some snow down her back. Fantine, for it is she, retaliates with an explosion of fury, scratching and swearing. Suddenly Javert makes his way through the crowd and peremptorily arrests her. At the police station, despite her pleas, he condemns her to six months in prison.

Without warning M. Madeleine enters and quietly interrupts the execution of the order. Fantine, still laboring under her mistaken impression of him, spits in his face. Undeterred, Madeleine carries through his merciful deed. Javert, of course, is stupefied by this outrage to authority and refuses to carry out his superior's order. It is only when the mayor explicitly invokes his authority that Javert is forced to set Fantine free. Fantine, before this titanic struggle that holds her fate in the balance, feels an upheaval in her soul. Finally, when

Madeleine promises her financial help and the return of her child she falls to her knees and faints.

Commentary

Fantine's degradation is skillfully portrayed, and every detail of Hugo's rather lengthy earlier description of her carries weight here, as the golden hair becomes a cropped stubble, the voluptuous lips give a gap-toothed grimace, and the dainty white blouse turns into a patched bodice topped by a dirty cap. The final touch of the snowball down the back is in the best traditions of realism, which involves us in the scene by an almost photographic accuracy of impression rather than by any commentary. By comparing M. Bamatabois and Félix Tholomyès in his essay on dandies, however, Hugo subtly underlines the point that Fantine's last torment, like her first, is the work of masculine vanity and callousness. The snowball incident was actually seen by Hugo in 1841. He waited over 20 years to find exactly the right place to use it in fiction.

The scene in the police office is again a graphic rather than a literary one, and in posing and lighting the three principal characters Hugo may have been influenced by a theme common in medieval painting — the struggle between an angel and a devil for the possession of a cringing soul. Indeed in their taste for local color and specific detail, as opposed to general truths, the Middle Ages and the nineteenth century are much alike.

Books VI-VIII

Summary

Fantine catches a high fever and Madeleine has her transported to the infirmary he has endowed. True to his word, he also writes the Thénardiers telling them to send Cosette. They, of course, sensing a profit, raise their financial demands; Madeleine immediately meets them. Unfortunately, Fantine is not getting better in spite of the nuns' devoted care. One day the doctor ominously recommends that Cosette be sent for as quickly as possible. Madeleine, armed with a note from Fantine, decides to get Cosette himself from the Thénardiers, who so far have stubbornly refused to give her up.

However, catastrophe is about to descend upon both Madeleine and Fantine. Unbeknown to the mayor, Javert has investigated Madeleine's past. Now Javert comes to see him with a surprising request: he wants to be relieved of his duties as inspector. He has in his own eyes committed an unpardonable transgression: he has accused Madeleine of being the ex-convict Jean Valjean. But the real Valjean has just been found; he now goes under the name of Champmathieu and has been arrested for stealing some apples by climbing the walls of an orchard and breaking off a branch. The identification is positive; not only has he been recognized by three of his fellow inmates, but Javert himself swears that the accused is Valjean. He is, in fact, leaving for Arras to testify at the trial, which is to take place the next day.

After Javert's departure, Valjean goes to the infirmary, stays with Fantine longer than usual, and recommends her to the special care of the nuns. Then he goes to a stable and rents a sturdy horse and carriage for 4:30 the next morning.

Until the arrival of the carriage he spends an agonizing, sleepless night. Irrationally he locks the door and blows out the candle. For one long hour, his head burning, he contemplates with horror the abyss into which he is about to slip. Then, with immense relief, he resolves to let fate have her way, to sacrifice Champmathieu to his own security. Later, however, the reproachful image of the bishop looms before him and he decides to give himself up. He puts his affairs in order, but the battle is not yet over: doubts and fearful visions weaken his resolve. He changes his mind again, this time even more definitely because the new solution seems morally right. He convinces himself that the welfare of many others — Fantine, Cosette, the whole town — depends on his staying out of prison. But his conscience returns to the assault, more imperious, more inflexible, until it seems like a real voice filling the room. For five endless hours he undergoes this torture, like Christ at Gethsemane.

At three o'clock he falls asleep, exhausted. But nightmarish dreams disturb his rest. He sees his dead brother, finds himself in a deserted village, among enigmatic crowds. He is abruptly awakened by his servant announcing the arrival of the carriage. For a moment he listens in an uncomprehending stupor. Then he says the fateful words: "All right, I'm coming down."

Driven by a mysterious compulsion, Valjean drives furiously to Arras. On the way, the wheels of a coach going in the opposite direction strike his, but he does not stop. At daybreak he has left Montreuil far behind. Several hours later he stops at Hesdin to feed his horse and let him rest, only to find out his wheel has been broken in the accident.

Valjean, however, will not give up. He wants to take the stagecoach. Impossible. He tries to borrow a horse. None available. He attempts to rent a carriage. There aren't any. Now he allows himself a long sigh of relief. He has done his best.

But fate has decided that he is not to be spared his tragic confrontation. Suddenly, an old woman approaches him and offers him an old wreck of a carriage. He accepts and goes on. Late in the evening after innumerable difficulties, Valjean reaches Arras.

At Arras, Valjean sets out for the courthouse. He makes his way through a crowd of sinister-looking lawyers and attempts to get into the courtroom. But the place is packed. There are only a few seats left behind the presiding judge reserved to public officials. Reluctantly, Valjean requests admission as mayor of Montreuil. Thanks to his widespread reputation, he is welcomed with great deference. He steps into the judge's chamber and, overcome by panic, flees, only to return once more with a sense of doom. Hypnotized by the copper handle of the door, he opens it like an automaton and finds himself in the courtroom. In the semi-darkness he discovers the accused and has the anguished vision of himself back in jail, a reversion to the degenerate and wretched creature he had been. Terrified, he sinks into a seat and hides his distress behind a pile of boxes.

Then he proceeds to watch the horrible spectacle of an innocent man crushed by the weight of evidence and the formidable apparatus of the law. Before the inexorable questions of the prosecutors, Champmathieu has only one pathetic defense: bewilderment.

Dramatically, the mayor interrupts the proceeding by confessing that he, and not Champmathieu, is Jean Valjean. He turns to the convicts and gives them such personal details about themselves that they are forced to recognize him. The audience is so stunned that nobody stops Madeleine-Valjean from leaving the courtroom; indeed, someone even opens the door for him.

Back in Montreuil, Valjean goes directly to the infirmary. Sister Simplicity is surprised by his unannounced arrival, but even more by his appearance, for his hair has turned snow white.

He enters Fantine's room and observes her thoughtfully while she sleeps. She, too, has changed. The approach of death has given her an ethereal glow, an inexpressible serenity. When she wakes up she looks at Madeleine without surprise and with a touching faith asks "And Cosette?" He mumbles an inadequate reply; luckily, the doctor comes to his aid and tells Fantine that her daughter is here but will not be allowed to visit her mother until Fantine feels better. The lie comforts Fantine, but with growing excitement she begins to talk about her daughter. Suddenly she stops and points behind Madeleine. He turns around and sees Javert, who with an expression of demoniac joy orders the mayor to come with him.

When Valjean fails to comply, the policeman grabs him by the collar. Valjean does not resist but, in a quiet voice, asks Javert privately for three days to go and bring back Cosette. Javert refuses, sneeringly and loudly, and Fantine realizes that her daughter has not arrived and that the mayor is a criminal under arrest. She suffers a convulsion and the shock kills her.

In Valjean's eyes, Javert has murdered her, and he is overcome by a terrible silent anger. Defying Javert, he says a silent goodbye to the dead woman and whispers a promise in her ear. Then he places himself at Javert's disposal.

The news of Valjean's arrest spreads quickly through Montreuil. The town to which he has brought prosperity unanimously rejects him. Only his old servant remains faithful. In the evening, as she sits musing over his tragedy, Valjean suddenly appears, explains that he has broken a bar of the jail window, and asks her to get Sister Simplicity. In his room, with closed shutters, he then packs up Little Gervais' coin and the bishop's candlesticks.

Sister Simplicity faithfully answers the summons and Javert, of course, follows soon after. In spite of the protestations of the servant, he resolutely climbs the stairs. Sister Simplicity falls to her knees and begins to pray, and continues to pray as Javert enters. His first impulse is to withdraw, but his professional conscience urges him on. Twice he asks the sister whether she has seen Valjean and twice she who has never lied answers "No." The categorical denial of such a holy person satisfies Javert and he insists no further.

An hour later, Valjean is walking quickly toward Paris. As for Fantine, she is thrown in a common grave to suffer the promiscuity of the dead as she had suffered the promiscuity of the living.

Commentary

Jean Valjean is sometimes spoken of as a "Christ figure," and Hugo, when he compares M. Madeleine's silent inner struggle with that in the Garden of Gethsemane, seems to underline this similarity, but it is not really an accurate comparison. Jean Valjean is a man from beginning to end and nowhere more human than here when he tries to use fate, accident, and his own responsibility to others as arguments to avoid his Calvary. Even when he does go to Arras, it is not so much the result of a conscious decision to sacrifice himself to another as out of the instinctive knowledge, which his dream has brought him, that if he does not go he will have no life left worth living. He will be spiritually dead.

The courtroom scene in which he declares his identity forms a perfect conclusion to Part One and is the exact counterpart of the meeting between Jean Valjean and the bishop early in the novel. Now, however, Champmathieu is the ignorant benighted victim persecuted by society, while Jean Valjean's suddenly white hair underlines the fact that he has inherited the saintliness of the Bishop of Digne.

PART TWO: COSETTE

Book I

Summary

Before resuming his story, Hugo acquaints the reader with such peripheral matters as the topography of Waterloo, a description of the farm of Hougomont, where Napoleon encountered his first setback, certain military considerations, and the emperor's personality.

Only then does the author launch into the long chronological narration of the Battle of Waterloo. It is the morning of June 18, 1815. In spite of the rain of the previous night which interferes with his plans, Napoleon exudes confidence. The army is in position, his strategy is decided. He gives the order to attack, expecting to deliver his usual stunning blow. But the British prove to be unusually stubborn opponents, and Napoleon suffers staggering losses in forcing Wellington to retreat on the Mont Saint Jean plateau.

The emperor orders Milhaud's cuirassiers, a formidable regiment 3,000 strong, to crush the enemy. Headed by Marshal Ney, they gallop like a massive juggernaut toward the British forces. But fate intervenes, putting in their path a sunken road impossible to detect from a distance. The troops fall headlong into it, carried on by their own impetus. Men and horses serve as a living bridge for their comrades to cross. The British assemble their artillery and proceed to shell the survivors.

The remainder of the regiment, however, continues the charge and hurls itself furiously on the enemy; in spite of the deadly calm efficiency of the British infantry, the regiment slices deep gaps in the British formations. Wellington orders his cavalry to attack from the rear, and suddenly the assailant becomes the defender, and the charge becomes a general slaughter. In one minute the cuirassiers lose 600 men, and the British formations are reduced from thirteen to seven.

Both sides are seriously weakened, but Wellington's losses are the greatest. His cavalry is destroyed, his artillery largely disabled, and panic begins to infect his ranks. At five o'clock, he is forced to the somber admission "Blucher [that is, reinforcement by the Prussian army which was supposed to join him earlier in the day] or the night."

Miraculously, a few minutes later, a line of bayonets sparkles on the horizon. Blucher's army, held up by the rains of the previous day, has arrived. This new intervention turns the tide of battle. Caught between Prussian shells and the bullets of the reinvigorated British, the French offensive turns into a rout, into disaster, into extermination.

Still the French do not succumb. Napoleon sends his picked troops, the Imperial Guard, against the British; marching resolutely against the enemy in the tide of universal retreat, it is mowed down rank by rank. Ultimately the whole Guard is destroyed: "Not one man misses his appointment with suicide." After this, panic is complete, and the French army turns into a disorganized mob which sweeps over the countryside pursued by Blucher's troops, who give no quarter.

One incident remains to be told, unimportant to the course of history, but illustrative of man's undying spirit. At the end of the battle an obscure officer named Cambronne is one of the few men still resisting. To the British exhortations to surrender he answers with one eloquently obscene word.

After the French defeat, the field is abandoned to the scavengers. Among the most industrious we find a certain Thénardier, who methodically proceeds to strip the dead. Suddenly a hand grabs him from behind. It is a dying officer clutching him for help. Calmly

Thénardier removes him from the cadavers and pockets his valuables. The officer, a man called Pontmercy, ironically believes Thénardier has saved his life and, asking his name, says he will never forget him.

Commentary

For some critics this description of the Battle of Waterloo is simply a typical example of nineteenth-century long-windedness, but in fact it is a vital part of *Les Misérables*. The society that persecutes Jean Valjean is not irrevocably cruel; it is capable of change, and of radical change in the interest of the poor and oppressed, as the Revolution showed. Napoleon I, dictator though he was, was a child of that Revolution and consolidated some of its liberal social advances. With his defeat at Waterloo and the consequent restoration of the Bourbons, social progress was checked; Jean Valjean, Fantine, Cosette, and thousands of others like them were again neglected. But their fate is not inevitable; history may again intervene to reverse the effects of Waterloo, and it is one of Hugo's purposes in writing *Les Misérables* to encourage it to do so.

Furthermore, Hugo uses the battle scene to warn us that his stage and his cast of characters is about to widen and that we shall meet not only characters from Book I, like Thénardier, but others yet unknown to us, of whom Pontmercy is the forerunner.

Finally, the epic quality of this book underlines the epic quality of the novel as a whole. The same capricious fate thwarts indifferently the plans of Napoleon I and M. Madeleine; the men of Waterloo and Jean Valjean struggle against their destinies with the same blind determination and terrible valor. From the moment when Hugo leads us, unsuspecting, through the gate of the farm of Hougomont with its brave bird singing and its banks of violets, we are in the hands of a great poet, who is as sensitive to the nuances of war as to those of everyday life and sees in both alike pity and horror, irony and beauty.

Book II

Summary

Valjean does not enjoy his freedom long. Several days after his prison break he is recaptured and sent to the galleys in Toulon. However, just a few days following Valjean's escape an incident takes place around Montfermeil that is not unrelated to our story. Every day an old roadworker, Boulatruelle, quits his job early and wanders in the most remote spots of the forest as if he were looking for something. To superstitious old women he is looking for the devil's treasure, for according to a legend, Satan has chosen the forest to hide his gold. A few skeptics, however, such as Thénardier — who is now innkeeper at Montfermeil — suspect that he is attracted by something more substantial than Satan's gold. Thénardier had the schoolmaster ply Boulatruelle with wine and extract a bit of intriguing information.

One morning as he was going to work, Boulatruelle had stumbled upon a hidden spade and pickaxe. Later, he had encountered a man whom he recognized as a fellow convict from years past, carrying a little chest. Interesting coincidence: the police had speculated that after his escape Jean Valjean had been in the vicinity of Montfermeil.

Toward the end of October of the same year, 1823, a ship docks at the Toulon shipyard for repairs. This routine operation is marred by a dramatic incident. A sailor working in the rigging high above the ship suddenly loses his footing and barely manages to avoid a fatal fall by grabbing a rope. But he remains in a perilous situation: incapable of climbing to the yard, he dangles like a stone at the end of a string. No one dares to help him and he seems doomed to plunge to his death.

Suddenly a convict, assigned to the ship, dashes to the riggings and climbs them with the agility of a cat. In a flash he is on the yard. For just a second he stops to gauge the distance to the end of the yard; then he runs to it, ties a rope around it, and lowers himself to the desperate man like a spider going after a fly. When he is within reach he attaches a rope to the sailor's body and lifts him to safety.

But the rescuer himself is not so fortunate. On the way back to his work gang he seems to lose his balance and drops into the sea. Four men immediately launch a boat to rescue him, but he has disappeared without leaving a trace. The next day the local papers announce Jean Valjean's death.

Commentary

The incident of Jean Valjean's heroic rescue of the sailor is taken from a friend's eyewitness account of a similar rescue by a convict which actually took place at Toulon. Writers of the Realistic school frequently took material from contemporary events — Flaubert's *Madame Bovary*, for instance, is based on a newspaper account of the suicide of a country doctor's wife—and Hugo in this same chapter uses fake newspaper reports to give "authenticity" to his account.

In fact the use of newspaper reports, false or true, in a novel does not necessarily add conviction. No amount of "real life" stuffing will save a novel that is not artistically and psychologically sound. But where the novel is otherwise satisfying, such devices do add powerfully to the *illusion* of authenticity.

Criminals sent to the galleys, as every reader of historical fiction knows, were used as oarsmen on those wooden men-of-war which, though they had sails, needed oar power to maneuver in a calm or in a crisis. The prisoners were exposed to every inclemency of weather and, chained to their benches, often went down with the ship. However, since such ships were outmoded early in the eighteenth century, it may surprise the reader to find Jean Valjean on one in 1823. In fact the "galériens" no longer ply the oars, but work for the navy shifting stores and repairing vessels at navy yards in Marseilles, Toulon, Rochefort, and Brest; and they sleep at night in shore prisons.

Book III

Summary

It is Christmas Eve at Montfermeil. At the Thénardier inn, the husband is drinking with the customers and the wife is supervising the meal. Cosette is at her usual place, huddled under the table near the chimney. Ragged and barelegged in her wooden shoes, she is knitting woolen socks for Eponine and Azelma, the Thénardier daughters. Upstairs a new Thénardier baby, a boy, is wailing; but his mother detests him and pays no attention.

Cosette muses somberly as she knits. Four travelers have arrived unexpectedly and she has had to fill their pitcher with water. That means the supply is probably exhausted, a situation fraught with anxiety for Cosette. She may have to go out in the black of night to fill the pail at the distant spring. Unfortunately, her worst fears are realized. A traveling salesman furiously complains that his horse has not been given anything to drink, and Mme. Thénardier consequently orders Cosette to bring back water. As an afterthought she hands her a coin to buy a loaf of bread.

The beginning of the trip is relatively reassuring, since the center of the town is filled with carnival stands whose candles give off a protective light. It even holds a brief and poignant pleasure. One of the shops contains a magnificent doll, which Cosette contemplates for a moment in delirious admiration.

But as she leaves the confines of the fair the night grows darker and the last glimmers of light vanish at the edge of the forest. The countryside is transformed into a nightmarish vision, a world of ghosts, animals, and unknown terrors. So great is Cosette's terror she does not notice her coin fall into the spring as she feverishly fills her pail.

The return trip is agonizingly slow. Every few steps she stops to put down her inhumanly heavy burden and rests. Suddenly the pail becomes weightless. A man has come up from behind and like a rescuing angel, has silently taken the handle from her grasp. A stranger just arrived from Paris, the man appears weary and grieved, and his clothes indicate a genteel poverty. After getting off the stagecoach, he has plunged into the forest instead of entering the village, and so has noticed Cosette.

The stranger accompanies her to the inn and on the way elicits her pathetic story. When she gives him her name, Cosette, he seems to receive a shock. When they arrive at the inn, on Cosette's timid suggestion he gives her back the pail to save her from a beating by the irascible Mme. Thénardier. Mme. Thénardier greets Cosette crossly and the stranger, on account of his unprepossessing appearance, with insolence. But he is indifferent to his reception and to the wine Cosette has automatically brought him; all his attention seems concentrated on the child.

Suddenly Mme. Thénardier remembers the bread. Cosette, desperately attempting to avoid her wrath, pretends the bakery was closed. But now she cannot find the coin to give it back. The stranger intervenes once more; pretending to pick up a coin from the floor, he gives the woman a 20-sou piece he has taken from his pocket. His kindness does not stop there. He notices that Cosette is diligently knitting while the Thénardier girls are playing without a care. Moved to compassion, he buys the unfinished socks for the exorbitant sum of five francs and relieves Cosette of her dreary task.

Little girls need toys to fill their leisure, however, and Cosette has none. When the Thénardier children abandon their doll for a moment to play with the cat, Cosette surreptitiously grabs it; but when the theft is discovered, Mme. Thénardier erupts with the violence of a storm.

Cosette wrings her hands in desperation and terror. The stranger then does an incredible thing. He steps out of the inn and returns with the magnificent doll from the village shop, which he hands to Cosette. The assembly is stunned, Mme. Thénardier is speechless, and Cosette contemplates the doll with awed veneration.

After his dramatic intervention, the man returns to his reverie and much later retires to his room, escorted by a now obsequious Thénardier. Before he retires, however, he performs one last good deed. The Thénardier girls have placed their little shoes near the chimney and a tender mother has put a 10-sou coin in each. Next to them stands a worn, muddy wooden shoe, empty. The traveler puts a shining gold louis in it and steals off to bed.

The next day the stranger reveals the purpose of his trip. He offers to relieve Mme. Thénardier of Cosette, and she eagerly accepts. Her husband, however, is more greedy. He plays the affectionate father, unwilling to abandon the child he cherishes. The stranger has to pay him 1,500 francs before he will relinquish her. The stranger takes Cosette's hand, and she trustingly follows him out of the inn.

But the happy ending is spoiled by one last complication. Egged on by his wife, the insatiable Thénardier runs after the pair to see if he can extort yet more money. Valjean — for of course it is he — plays his trump card and shows the innkeeper Fantine's note. When Thénardier still tries to follow from a distance, Valjean raises his cane menacingly and disappears into the forest with his precious charge.

Commentary

Once again the Thénardiers appear in our story, and we realize that they are and will remain an integral part of the novel. In contrast to Jean Valjean, who represents man rising from animality to sainthood, the Thénardiers are losing their humanity and becoming savage brutes. In describing them, Hugo uses the common realistic and naturalistic technique of presenting selected details of external appearance, and letting these suggest the truth of the inner man. By the time he has finished painting Mme. Thénardier's stature, her energy, her great voice, her freckles, her beard, and her jutting tooth, we can see for ourselves she is a monster, and Hugo does not need to tell us so.

With the innkeeper, Hugo extends his exploration somewhat beyond Thénardier's surface appearance. He adds details of manner, gesture, and speech that are characteristic of the man, and he even goes so far as to say Thénardier is a hypocritical crook. None of these facts, however, goes beyond what a shrewd observer might deduce about the innkeeper on modest acquaintance, and Hugo is very careful never to take us "inside" Thénardier. "We believe," he says about the details of the man's past; it is a guess, not a statement; and he concludes, "There was some mystery in Thénardier." It is just this, in fact, that makes him so terrifying a personage.

As for Cosette, Hugo sums up the history of her last five years in terms of the most common and vivid of childhood experiences – fear of the dark. The intensity of her fear is so great, however, that we recognize without being told that it is the expression of a thousand other unexpressed real terrors. Her fear of the night is only the outward mark of the fear kindled in her by her total solitude and inhuman treatment.

There were many such abandoned children in nineteenth-century France, rejects of an industrialized society that no longer had any use for them. Fantine herself was an abandoned child, and like Cosette, her name meant only "little one"; but she was raised by the village to which she belonged because in an agricultural society a child can always earn its keep: tend sheep, feed chickens. In the nineteenth-century city, however, there was no way for a small child to help carry the family's economic burden, and it was often abandoned to allow the parents to work.

Cosette is fortunate that she is useful at the inn; for Mme. Thénardier has exactly the temperament of those infamous nineteenth-century baby-nurses who, when their payment for the care of an unwanted baby did not come, promptly tied the infant up in brown paper and dropped it in a river.

Hugo has compensations for Cosette, however. Her St. Nicholas may be only an old convict, but he comes with exactly the right fairy-tale gifts – the biggest doll in the world and a gold piece down the chimney. What is more, her Christmas miracle is to be a lasting one. It is one of the oldest stories in the world Hugo tells here, but it is always a satisfying one.

Book IV—
Book V, Chapters 1-5

Summary

In Paris, Valjean takes refuge in a dilapidated house in an outlying district. The only other tenant is an old woman who also performs the functions of caretaker. Passing off Cosette as his granddaughter and himself as a bourgeois ruined by unlucky investments, he lives quietly and at last happily. He lavishes on the little girl his immense reservoir of long-suppressed affection and she responds with equal love. He teaches her to read or simply watches her undress her doll. Cosette plays, chatters, and sings.

The world seems to have forgotten Jean Valjean, but he continues to take infinite precautions. He only goes out at night, sometimes with Cosette, sometimes alone, always choosing back alleys and deserted neighborhoods. His only contact with society is a visit to church or giving charity to a beggar.

He does not, however, remain undisturbed long. The old caretaker, tirelessly inquisitive, watches his every move. One day through a crack in the door she catches him taking a 1,000-franc bill from the lining of his coat. A moment later he approaches her and asks her to go change it, saying it is a dividend he has just received. But as he only goes out at night after the post office is closed, his explanation is highly suspicious. A few days later the room is momentarily deserted and the old woman creeps in to examine the intriguing coat. The lining is filled with paper — no doubt more bills — and the pockets with such incriminating objects as needles, scissors, and a collection of wigs.

On his nightly walks, Valjean has regularly been giving a few cents to an old beggar who sits at a nearby well. One evening as Valjean is ready to give his customary alms, the beggar raises his head and Valjean, petrified, seems to see the familiar face of Javert. The next night he returns to confirm his suspicion, but it is the same harmless beggar he knows from before.

However, in the evening a few days later Valjean hears the front door open and shut, and someone climbs the stairs to stand in front of his door. The next morning he hears footsteps again and through the keyhole sees Javert's formidable silhouette. That evening he makes a roll of his ready cash and taking Cosette by the hand, departs from the lodgings.

Commentary

A nineteenth-century novel is meant to be savored slowly, not rushed through to find out "what happens next"; and Chapter 1 of Book IV is a good example of the pleasures it can offer a reader willing to linger. Not only does Hugo give us a fascinating historical portrait of a section of Paris in 1823 and again in the 1860s, and a perceptive and witty comment on the magical swiftness with which faster transportation changes the look and feel of our environment, but a poetic evocation of a particular type of city area—a "hell of monotony"—which still fits perfectly our interstitial areas today with their rows of concrete gas stations, used car and trailer lots, and neon signs.

Hugo's city, however, is never truly urban, never the dense center of commercial and social relationships we find portrayed in Balzac or Zola. If Hugo's nature sometimes—as with Cosette at the spring—seems to take on the attributes of a person, his city equally often takes on the aspect of the countryside. When Jean Valjean needs a banker, he relies on a tree; but conversely, the maze of Paris streets is for him a jungle whose trees are lampposts and whose clearings are squares. There are times when Hugo sees Paris still with the eyes of the boy who grew up across from the Feuillantines Park in the middle of the city —as a wonderful place in which to play hide and seek.

Book V, Chapters 6-10

Summary

Jean Valjean maneuvers through the back streets of Paris like a hunted deer. He has no destination, no plan; he simply wants to throw Javert off the scent. Instead of leading him to freedom, his labyrinthine escape route brings him to a police station, where Javert picks up three allies and gives the alarm.

Valjean beats a hasty retreat and momentarily confuses his pursuers. When he reaches the Austerlitz Bridge he is detained at the tollgate and consequently observed by the gatekeeper. He continues his headlong flight, but Cosette's exhaustion impedes his progress. Then, tragically, he is trapped. The street he is following forms a "T" with another street, terminating on the right in a dead end and barred on the left by a police lookout. Behind him, invisible but terribly present, Javert inexorably advances.

Frantically casting around for an avenue of escape, Valjean notices a vast building which might possibly serve as a refuge. But the windows are barred, the pipes rickety, the doors unyielding. In his desperation, he decides to climb the walls, and miraculously finds a rope to aid him — the rope that lowers and raises the gas street-lanterns so that they can easily be lit. He cuts it, ties it around Cosette's body, takes the other end between his teeth, throws his shoes and socks over the wall, and then climbs it like a cat-burglar at the spot where the wall forms an angle with another building.

When he reaches the top, he pulls Cosette up, jumps on the roof of a building leaning against the wall, clambers down what appears to be a linden tree, and winds up in a garden. Outside Javert's voice barks imperative orders. The garden in which Valjean has arrived is vast and depressing. He distinguishes a big building with barred windows and, in the distance, the silhouette of other buildings. Suddenly an eerie sound breaks the silence, a hymn sung by an ethereal choir.

The winter wind begins to blow and Cosette shivers; Valjean wraps her in his own coat and then starts out to explore the grounds. As he peers through one of the windows, a macabre sight paralyzes him with terror. In a deserted room a human form is lying prone on the floor, motionless, covered with a shroud, its arms in the shape of a cross.

He returns to Cosette panting with fright, and sits down next to her; she has fallen asleep. His loving contemplation of the child is broken by the ringing of a little bell and he sees a man limping alone in a melon patch, bending and rising rhythmically, accompanied by the sound of the bell. Valjean has no time to examine the mystery, for he suddenly notices that Cosette's hands are nearly frozen. She is not dead, as he at first fears, but her breathing is shallow. There is obviously an urgent need to find her warmth and a bed.

Valjean does not hesitate. He goes straight to the man in the garden and shouts to him, "A hundred francs if you give us shelter for the night." Unexpectedly, the stranger answers, "Well! It's you, M. Madeleine!" and continues to chat with Valjean like an old friend. Valjean, astonished, recognizes Fauchelevent, the old man whose life he saved when he was trapped under a cart. Fauchelevent explains that they are in the garden of the convent of Petit-Picpus, where he is gardener. He is still very grateful to "M. Madeleine" for saving his life, and left Montreuil before Valjean's true identity was discovered, so he readily agrees not only to keep Valjean's secret, but to harbor him and Cosette.

A warm bed in his cottage brings Cosette back to consciousness, and a glass of wine and a frugal meal revive Valjean.

While they rest, Hugo explains Javert's uncanny arrival on the scene. There is really no mystery about it. When Valjean "drowned," the police suspected he might really have escaped and would, like many fugitives, head for Paris. Javert was called to Paris to assist with the hunt because he knew Valjean by sight, and his subsequent zeal and intelligence earned him an appointment to the Paris police force. Some time later, Javert came upon the report of the kidnaping of a little girl from her guardians, the Thénardiers, at Montfermeil. He suspected it was Jean Valjean who had taken Cosette away and subsequently learned that at the Gorbeau House there lived an old bourgeois whose "granddaughter" came from Montfermeil. Thoroughly suspicious now, he disguised himself as the old beggar one evening and identified Jean Valjean.

Commentary

Once again we see Jean Valjean fleeing, as he fled from Digne and from Montreuil; but this time something in his silhouette is different—he is carrying a child as he flees. No longer the solitary thief, he takes on the appearance of a St. Christopher, a man defined not by what he is but by what he carries and how he bears his burden. But as Hugo points out, Jean Valjean's burden is in itself its own reward. In taking on Cosette, he expects responsibility, but what he gets is love. Jean Valjean may be an apprentice saint, but as a social human being he is stunted because his criminal past has cut him off from the society of others. Cosette too has been stunted by cruelty and neglect. Together, however, they can form their own society and expand in heart and soul through the experience of loving each other.

Throughout Part Two Hugo's palette is somber, and in both the episode of Cosette's trip to the well and that of the "night hunt" we have scenes of darkness only fitfully touched by light which resemble the scene in the bishop's bedroom in Part One. However there is a contrast in mood and movement between the two darkness scenes in Part Two. The total darkness at the well is sinister, and Cosette escapes it by moving into the moonlight where she meets Jean Valjean, then into the firelight at the inn where he protects her. In the "night hunt," it is the fitful moments of light which reveal Jean Valjean to his pursuers that are sinister, and the total darkness into which he plunges on the other side of the wall in the Rue Droit Mur spells safety.

Books VI-VII

Summary

Hugo pauses in his story to give a long description of the convent in whose garden Jean Valjean now finds himself: its founding, its inhabitants, its activities, even the colors in which its walls are painted. In the chapter following, he gives his own personal views on the subject of monastic institutions.

Commentary

Because, according to the tenets of realism, environment is one of the most important factors in forming character, a detailed description of the character's environment is common. Hugo had all the details he gives us here about convent life from Juliette Drouet; they are all accurate, and for someone interested in convent life, even fascinating. But fifty pages of convent is, for the ordinary reader, far too much.

Hugo does have two practical aims, however, in discussing the convent at length. He wants us to understand thoroughly this atmosphere, which will add its gift of humility to the charity Bishop Myriel taught Jean Valjean and which for so many years will protect Cosette's innocence while not depriving her entirely of feminine mischief such as eating forbidden fruit (the orchard apples and pears) and reading forbidden books (the Rules of St. Benedict.)

He also, in an age when a single church and a Divine Monarchy still vie for French loyalty with an irreligious democracy, wishes to state his position on the religious question. Hugo as a modern man finds convents unnatural and unproductive, but as a poet, he cannot help admiring the sublimity of the monastic sacrifice. And if the convent stultifies, so does pure materialism: there is no Progress without an Ideal. What he himself would prefer is a more active, a more secular form of salvation, the striving for social utopia.

Book VIII

Summary

Valjean realizes that with Javert back on his trail he is lost if he goes back into the outside world. It is imperative that he remain in the convent. But even with Fauchelevent's loyal assistance the difficulties are insuperable. He cannot wander very far in this community of women. He cannot even stay hidden, for the convent has boarding students, whose tireless curiosity would soon betray the fugitives. Valjean's only hope is to be officially accepted by the nuns under some plausible alias. But to return in a normal way, he must first leave the convent undetected.

Both men fruitlessly examine the problem until Fauchelevent is summoned by the prioress. She gives him a confidential mission. A nun, Sister Crucifixion, has died that morning. Her last wish was to be buried in the vault under the altar. As this is against the law, a bit of subterfuge is required to carry out her request. The prioress asks Fauchelevent to come back before midnight, after the coroner's visit, to nail down the coffin and bury it in the vault. Later he is to accompany an earth-filled casket to the cemetery to throw the authorities off the track. As he listens to the instructions, Fauchelevent, who is not without peasant shrewdness, has been suggesting that he has a brother who could usefully help him in the garden and a niece who might become a nun if she were allowed to go to school at the convent. Satisfied with Fauchelevent's cooperation, the prioress gives him permission to bring his supposed brother and niece to the convent to live.

When Fauchelevent tells Jean Valjean what has just taken place, the ex-convict has a hair-raising idea. He himself will occupy the false casket, and at the cemetery Fauchelevent can get his friend Mestiennes, the gravedigger, drunk and free Valjean. As for Cosette, she will simply be carried out by Fauchelevent in a basket on his back.

The next day at sunset Fauchelevent confidently follows the funeral procession to the Vaugirard cemetery. Everything is going well and Valjean's confident courage has reassured him. At the gate an unexpected *contretemps* strikes him like a thunderbolt. He is greeted not by the alcoholic Mestienne, but by a replacement, Gribier; Mestienne has just died. In his bewilderment, Fauchelevent can think of nothing better than to continue with the original plan, but the new gravedigger is a teetotaler and virtuously refuses Fauchelevent's repeated urgings to come and have a drink with him.

Valjean has weathered his ordeal well, has suffered stoically through the long procession, the descent into the grave, and finally the lugubrious funeral services. But when he hears the earth falling on the casket and understands its implications, he faints.

Above ground, desperation has brought inspiration to Fauchelevent. He has noticed a white card in the gravedigger's pocket, his pass to enter and leave the cemetery after sunset. Fauchelevent steals the pass skillfully, then brings the loss to his companion's attention. Gribier is terrified, for the loss incurs a large fine. Fauchelevent helpfully suggests he go home and look for it, offering to guard the grave. The gravedigger, overwhelmed with gratitude, shakes his hand and dashes away. Valjean is soon freed and the fake burial completed. The two men leave the cemetery without further difficulty.

An hour later, two men and a little girl present themselves at the gate of the convent. Valjean makes a good impression on the prioress, and Cosette's homeliness seems to predestine her to become a nun. Valjean is installed as assistant gardener and Cosette is accepted as a student. Life for Valjean is henceforth to be confined within the walls of the convent, but he is satisfied with it. His work gives him serenity and he finds consolation in Cosette's daily visits. She too is happy. Laughter, like sunshine, dissipates the winter in her heart. In this fashion, several years go by.

Commentary

Part Two as a whole has presented technical problems for Hugo. Its plot comprises only three events: Valjean's escape and rescue of Cosette; his flight from Javert; and his discovery of a new refuge in the convent. This is very little action to stretch over nearly 300 pages, and Hugo uses various devices to maintain the reader's interest: cumulative suspense, deliberate mystifications, and unexpected dramatic confrontations only later explained in flashbacks.

When Jean Valjean comes to the inn, there is no real reason why he cannot simply present Fantine's note and take Cosette away directly. Instead, Hugo has him approach the problem in a subtler manner, so that for several chapters the reader does not know whether he will succeed in rescuing the child or not. Interest is sustained, and the rescue when it comes is much more emotionally satisfying.

Hugo also deliberately mystifies us at three points in Part Two. Valjean falls from the mast at Toulon, but it is a long time before we are quite sure that he has survived and made good his escape. Boulatruelle suspects a man of burying treasure in the woods, but again we do not know for sure that it is Valjean, and that he has secreted the wealth he gained as M. Madeleine, until much later in the book. And finally, the strange sights and sounds Valjean sees after he has climbed over the wall into the convent garden are deliberately chosen to alarm and puzzle us, and to pique our curiosity.

The flashback is a legitimate dramatic device, almost as old as the novel itself, and Hugo uses it here and in many other places in *Les Misérables* to good effect. To explain Javert's appearance immediately he enters upon the scene would be to weaken all the dramatic effect of his irruption into Valjean and Cosette's peaceful life and would destroy the unity and steadily mounting suspense of the discovery-chase-escape sequence. As it is, crisis follows crisis until Valjean disappears over the convent wall; and then, satisfied that he is safe, we are prepared to hear an explanation of Javert's presence.

The suspense in Chapter 8 is also very effectively maintained, and the working out of a complex criminal escape plot against the background of a convent also gives Hugo an opportunity for one of the dramatic contrasts both he and the reader enjoy.

PART THREE: MARIUS

Book I

Summary

Hugo opens this section with a sentimental tribute to the Parisian gamin, or street urchin. The gamin is for him a pearl of innocence hidden under outer depravity and squalor. He uses slang, talks to prostitutes, frequents bars, wears rags, sings obscene ditties, and sneers at religion. Yet for all his apparent immorality he elicits admiration. His skepticism mocks sham and convention. It is served by a lively wit and a picturesque vocabulary. At times, when he is sufficiently aroused, the gamin rises to the sublime. To use Hugo's image, this handful of mud becomes Adam when it is sparked by the divine breath. And he is happy in spite of his wretched poverty. The street is for him an everexciting domain full of marvels, fraught with adventures. In the evening he loses himself in the magic of the theater.

Nine years have elapsed since the events related in the second part. Hugo now introduces Gavroche, a boy of eleven or twelve — gay, free, hungry, slightly larcenous, dressed in hand-me-downs, a typical Parisian urchin. There is a tragic background to his life, however. He has been callously abandoned by his parents, brutally kicked out of the nest. Yet in spite of the estrangement, every few months he goes to see his mother in the Gorbeau House. The visit is invariably depressing. Gavroche is greeted by abysmal poverty, hunger, and worse, indifference. The conversation is laconic and matter-of-fact:

— Where have you come from?
— The street.
— Where are you going?
— Back to the street.
— Why did you come?

Commentary

By now we are used to Hugo's dramatic technique of shifting us abruptly from the known to the unfamiliar, in a plot dislocation that is more apparent than real, and we are confident that if we are patient he will eventually bring us back to Jean Valjean.

The problem of the abandoned child has already been evoked with Cosette. Hugo reverts to it here by introducing Gavroche, who is — in more ways than one, as we shall see — a sort of little brother to Cosette but even more unlucky than she. Where misfortune stupefied her, however, it has only sharpened Gavroche's wits.

In 1830 the average life expectancy of a bourgeois' child was eight years; of a worker's, two. This statistic goes a long way to explain the phenomenon of the Paris gamin: those children who survive parental neglect and the urban death rate have already proved themselves remarkably flexible and sturdy and are, in a sense, the pick of the crop. With keen observation and tender empathy Hugo portrays their courage and their sufferings, their irreverence and their audacity, and glorifies them as symbols of that spirit which makes Paris the capital of the world. And finally, he uses them as a telling argument in favor of universal schooling; if they, unlettered, show so much ingenuity, intelligence, and wit, what could they not achieve with education?

Books II-III

Summary

In the neighborhood around the Temple there lives a curious character. M. Gillenormand, vestige of another age. His ninety years have in no way diminished his vigor. He walks straight, drinks with gusto, speaks loudly, sleeps soundly, snores vigorously. He has given up women, but not without some lingering regrets. When a former maid in the house tries to claim he is the father of her baby boy, he flatly denies it, but pays for the child's keep just the same, and for that of his little brother later on.

He is authoritarian and cannot brook contradiction. He still beats his servants in the grand old tradition and even punishes his fifty-year-old unmarried daughter. He has retained the Enlightenment's cynicism about the world. Europe, to him, is a civilized version of the jungle. Of course, he finds contemporary society particularly repulsive. He declares peremptorily: "The Revolution is a bunch of rascals."

M. Gillenormand has outlived most of his relatives. He still has, as we have just mentioned, an old maid daughter, a lackluster creature. In her youth she dreamed of a rich husband, prominence, an imposing butler. Now she has turned into a prude and a bigot. She defends with a heavy fortress of clothing an unthreatened virtue. She fills her day with religious practices, says special prayers, belongs to the Association of the Virgin, and venerates the Sacred Heart. She is, moreover, abominably stupid.

Her younger sister, now dead, was her exact opposite. She breathed poetry, flowers and light, dreamed of falling in love with a remote heroic cavalier, and married the man of her dreams. She has left behind a son, Marius, who lives with M. Gillenormand. Marius is a sensitive child who trembles before his gruff grandfather, for the latter speaks to him severely and sometimes raises his cane to him. Secretly, however, M. Gillenormand adores the child.

Even though the boy lives under his grandfather's care he is not an orphan. His father lives in very straitened circumstances in the little town of Vernon. Practically a hermit, he has only one occupation: the cultivation of a magnificent garden.

This humble and peaceful retirement, however, is the poignant conclusion to a stormy existence. The father, Georges Pontmercy, was for most of his life a soldier in Napoleon's army. He had a heroic career, distinguishing himself in all the Emperor's campaigns. He captured a British ship, was severely wounded, and won the highest military decoration. At the debacle of Waterloo he achieved the peak of valor by capturing the flag of the Lunebourg battalion. The emperor, delighted, shouted, "I'm making you a colonel, a baron, an officer of the Legion of Honor."

The Restoration did not look with favor on one of Napoleon's staunchest partisans, and Pontmercy was retired on half pay. Worse, the reactionary M. Gillenormand detests him, calls him a "bandit" and pressures him into giving up his son under the threat of disinheriting the child. Marius knows that he has a father, but he is completely indifferent to him. From the disapproval his name evokes in his royalist environment, he has gathered that his father is a man to be ashamed of.

He is tragically mistaken. Georges Pontmercy was not only a heroic soldier, he is a loving father. Unable to bear total separation from his child, he periodically comes to Paris and stealthily enters St. Sulpice church to watch his son at mass. His sacrifice has brought him a small consolation. It has won him the friendship of the curate of Vernon, M. l'abbé Mabeuf. This priest is a brother of the churchwarden of St. Sulpice, who has noticed Pontmercy, his scars, and his tears, during his secret visits to the church. On a visit to his brother at Vernon, Mabeuf recognizes Pontmercy; the two brothers pay the colonel a visit and learn his story. This confidence has created a friendship based on mutual admiration.

In 1827, Marius has just turned seventeen. One evening as he comes home his grandfather hands him a letter.

— Marius, says M. Gillenormand, you are to go to Vernon tomorrow.
— Why?
— To see your father.

The colonel is ill and has asked to see his son. Marius is not anxious to go, because he feels that his father has deserted him. Nevertheless he sets out for Vernon the next day. He is too late, however. Georges Pontmercy is dead. Marius is not grief-stricken: he feels only the sadness caused by the death of any stranger. He leaves 48 hours later, taking with him a note, his only legacy from his father.

The note reads, "To my son: The Emperor named me baron on the battlefield of Waterloo. Since the Restoration questions the title I won with my blood, my son will take it and bear it. It goes without saying that he will be worthy of it." On the back, the colonel adds: "At the same battle of Waterloo, a sergeant saved my life. The man is called Thénardier. Lately I believe he has been running an inn in the vicinity of Paris in Chelles or Montfermeil. If my son meets him he will be as helpful as he can."

One day Marius' indifference to his father is shaken by a fortuitous encounter with the churchwarden who knew and admired Georges Pontmercy. A casual conversation brings Marius the momentous revelation of his father's selfless love and the explanation of his apparent neglect. Marius is stunned. The next day he asks his grandfather's permission to leave for three days. What he does will be explained later. On his return he goes straight to the library and asks for the collection of the newspaper *Le Moniteur*. He devours it and everything else he can read concerning the Republic and the Empire. He hardly ever comes home. The old man, judging from his own past, suspects a love affair. It *is* something of the sort. Marius has begun to worship his father.

His emotional upheaval is accompanied by a transformation in his political views. The Revolution which in the past seemed to him one of the darkest chapters of history now impresses him with its battle for civil rights for the masses; the Empire becomes the standard-bearer of democracy in Europe. Likewise, Marius reconsiders his ideas about Napoleon, who ceases to be the monster of Marius' childhood and is transformed into the victorious captain who swept away the last remnants of the Old Regime. One stormy night, overwhelmed by the majesty of the hour, Marius completes his conversion by the fervent exclamation, "Long live the Emperor!" He is now entirely his father's son; he goes to a printer on the Quai des Orfevres and orders visiting cards with the inscription "Baron Marius Pontmercy."

At the same time, Marius draws away from his grandfather. He has always found him uncongenial; now his dislike becomes more specific. He blames the old man for the stupid prejudice that deprived him of a father's love. He becomes distant and cold, and frequently takes short trips away from home. During one of these he goes to look for Thénardier, his father's rescuer. But Thénardier has gone bankrupt, the inn is closed, and its owner has disappeared.

Marius' periodic absences have aroused the curiosity of Mlle. Gillenormand, especially since she scents a juicy scandal. She sends another nephew, Theodule, who has never met his cousin, to find out what Marius is doing. Théodule does not obey, but accidentally finds himself on the same coach and travels with Marius to Vernon.

At Vernon, both young men get off the coach, and Marius buys a beautiful bouquet from a flower vendor. Théodule follows him, expecting to observe a tender rendezvous. Instead he finds a somber tête-à-tête with a tomb. Marius has taken his flowers to a cross on which is inscribed the name, "Colonel Baron Pontmercy."

Théodule does not report what he has learned, but later on, M. Gillenormand investigates Marius' room and discovers Pontmercy's note to his son and the visiting cards. When Marius returns, there is a heated confrontation and bitter words are exchanged, words too bitter to be forgotten. Marius leaves his home forever. With 30 francs in his pocket, his watch, a few clothes, and only vague plans in mind, he sets out for the Latin Quarter.

Commentary

M. Gillenormand is an exceptional human being, as tough for an old man as Gavroche for a gamin, but in quite a different social sphere. Gavroche belongs to the slums of the nineteenth century, the octogenarian to the salons of the eighteenth, and everything about him, from his profanity to his bed hangings, breathes the atmosphere of another age. He has all the virtues of the eighteenth-century upper classes—their elegance, gaiety, and charm—and their worst failing, callous class egoism. M. Gillenormand is not, however, cruel or mean; he is generous with money, kind enough to support two bastards who are not even his, and in fact he and his grandson are very much alike. Unfortunately, their differences grate on particularly sensitive points. Marius' attitude to his fellow man, as we shall see, is more fraternal than patriarchal; he believes it is a virtue to feel strongly, while M. Gillenormand thinks it is in bad taste; and the egoism of youth is as stubborn as the egoism of age.

Even so, no separation would have come between them except for an accident of history. M. Gillenormand has an emotional horror of everything that has to do with the Revolution, and Marius cannot endure to deny a second time a father he has already involuntarily neglected. Like many Frenchmen of their age, Marius and his grandfather suddenly and unhappily find themselves on opposite sides of the widening chasm between the Old Regime and the young Republic.

Book IV

Summary

As his cab takes him without destination through the streets of the Latin Quarter, Marius is hailed by a fellow student, Bossuet. He tells him of his difficulties, but Bossuet though full of goodwill, is unable to help, since he himself is homeless. Another classmate, Courfeyrac, however, comes to the rescue and suggests a room in the Hotel de la Porte Saint Jacques, where he himself lives. With the spontaneity of youth, the two students immediately become friends.

This friendship is to have a profound effect on Marius' intellectual life. Courfeyrac belongs to a radical group, the Friends of the A.B.C. (This is a serious pun; the pronunciation of A.B.C. in French is the same as *abaissé*, the oppressed.) Inevitably, he introduces his new friend and Marius is caught up in a tide of new ideas. Nothing is respected in these wild and irreverent discussions. Not even Napoleon is spared. When the word "crime" is applied to his empire, Marius, usually reserved, explodes in a passionate harangue and eloquently defends Napoleon's career. But his concluding question, "What is greater than Napoleon's conquests?" is squelched by a quiet retort, "To be free."

Marius' new convictions are shaken, but not enough to make him embrace the more radical ideas expounded around him. He suffers from intellectual uncertainty and isolation. Material difficulties aggravate his unhappiness. He has no job and he proudly refuses help from home. To pay his most pressing bills he sells his few possessions and leaves the hotel. These measures are mere palliatives, however.

Commentary

Having reassured us somewhat by explaining the Colonel Pontmercy who appeared out of nowhere in Part Two, and by connecting Marius with him, Hugo now takes us to meet yet a third group of unknown characters, the Friends of A.B.C. However, all these strangers — Gavroche, Marius, Enjolras and his friends, and even M. Mabeuf of Book V — are only apparently introduced at random. All their destinies are converging on one historic moment where they will also become entangled with the fate of Jean Valjean.

Hugo describes each member of the student group with affection and understanding; and the assortment of temperaments he portrays — Enjolras the militant, Combeferre the genial philosopher, Prouvaire the artistic idealist, Feuilly the intelligent workman, Courfeyrac the "good guy," Bahorel the irrepressible, Bossuet (Laigle) and Joly the misfits, and Grantaire the cynic — can be duplicated in student activist groups today. Enjolras is a particularly interesting study, since he is one of the first portrayals in literature of that characteristic nineteenth-century

58

angel of death, the political idealist, the flawless fanatic, the "pure" Marxist or anarchist. What really justifies the attention Hugo devotes to these young men, however, is that they are all going to die.

It will be noted that Marius' political evolution follows that of Hugo himself—from the royalism of his Breton mother to the mildly liberal Bonapartism of his heroic father to a firm devotion to Republican principles.

Books V-VI

Summary

After he exhausts his last resources, Marius finds life cruel. He suffers in body and soul. He has no bread and no fire, and his clothes are shabby. He bears the insolence of shopkeepers, the laughter of working girls, taunts, humiliation. At one point his coat wears out and he has to accept cast-offs from his friends. But poverty is a crucible that destroys the weak and tempers the soul of the strong. Marius proves himself firm in the face of adversity and slowly manages to create a bearable existence. He earns a modest living as a literary factotum, writing prospectuses, annotating editions, translating newspapers, and compiling biographies. He lives in a monkish room in the Gorbeau House—the same building once occupied by Cosette and Jean Valjean. He eats frugally and never drinks wine.

Marius is at peace with the world, for his austere way of life is in keeping with his ascetic temperament. He lives like a hermit, avoiding even his own family. Unaware that his grandfather secretly regrets his behavior, Marius never goes to see him. He has given up his circle of student friends, cultivating only Courfeyrac and the old churchwarden, M. Mabeuf, who knew his father. Solitude suits him. It allows him to abandon himself to a life of contemplation that provides him with moments of veritable ecstasy. Marius is in the process of becoming a visionary.

Consequently, he is completely indifferent to any woman whom chance puts in his path. For a year now on his regular walks in the Luxembourg Gardens he has frequently encountered an old man with a pleasant countenance and the modest air of a Quaker, accompanied by a little girl thirteen or fourteen years old. Marius is favorably impressed by the "father," but finds the "daughter" of no interest.

Then, for no particular reason, he interrupts his visits to the park and does not see the unknown couple for six months. A momentous event has taken place during his absence. The ugly duckling has become a swan, and the little girl has become a ravishing young woman. So striking is the transformation that Marius has to observe her attentively to make sure it is the same person. Yet this new beauty does not at first dispel his indifference.

Later, however, their eyes meet, and Marius' whole life changes. In this one glance he finds a depth, a mystery, a charm, that intoxicates him. Suddenly he is ashamed of his old clothes, and the next day he appears at the Luxembourg Gardens resplendent in his new suit. Resolute, proud of his appearance, he walks toward the bench on which the young girl sits with her father. As he draws near, however, his emotions overwhelm him and he has to turn back. Once again, he attempts the difficult adventure and this time manages to pass the bench, but not without acute embarrassment. Then he sits down at a respectable distance, and a quarter of an hour later, leaves in a trance. That night he forgets to have supper.

For two weeks he continues to stroll past the bench, nothing more. Then a cataclysmic event takes place. M. Leblanc, as Marius has decided to call the old man on account of his white hair, decides to take his daughter for a walk and they stroll in front of Marius. Ineffable moment: he is dazzled by the pensive and gentle look she gives him. Her beauty reminds him of an angel, of the heroines of Petrarch and Dante. He is floating on clouds and painfully aware of the dust on his boots.

When he is not in the Luxembourg Gardens, Marius is, like all lovers, afflicted with a touch of madness. He is alternately thoughtful and uproariously gay. He embraces strangers. He makes remarks out of context. A whole month goes by, and he never misses a day at the Luxembourg. But restrained by timidity and caution, he does not again parade in front of the bench. With apparent casualness, he stands near a statue or tree, exhibiting himself to the young girl and sending her tender looks. She, in turn, manages to return his glances with meaningful looks of her own while talking to her father.

A few miscalculations, however, put an end to Marius' discreet courtship. One day M. Leblanc changes benches and Marius follows. Then he comes without his daughter and Marius, by leaving immediately, makes it obvious that he has been interested in her. He has picked up a handkerchief initialed "U" which he thinks she has dropped, and he has christened her "Ursula" in his private thoughts; and finally he tries to follow "Ursula" to her home. This last mistake is irreparable. He asks the doorman about her; the doorman tells "M. Leblanc" of the inquiry; and a week later, the old man and the girl have disappeared without a trace.

Commentary

The description of how Marius lives on 700 francs a year is a passage straight out of Balzac's type of realism, and it has all the mathematical fascination of a well-worked-out equation. Marius however is not, and never will be, one of Les Misérables. Unlike Gavroche and Jean Valjean, he does not expect suffering from life; he chooses it, and thereby adds a halo of glory to the rosy glow of youth that already surrounds him. Marius' natural environment is not the slums but the Luxembourg Gardens; he belongs to the world of the wealthy, the leisured, the fortunate, and no matter how shabby his pants, he always wears them like a gentleman.

In Marius, Victor Hugo is painting his own portrait as a young man —the same political views, appearance, and youthful struggles—but it is a fair portrait, unretouched. Hugo recognizes what is admirable in Marius—his integrity, his generosity, his imaginative fervor, his genuine idealism, and his capacity for feeling; but he does not extol them beyond measure, and he does not fail to point out Marius' faults: the unconscious cruelty with which he makes his grandfather suffer and the humor as well as the beauty of his grand passion. To fall in love forever, without a word spoken, on the strength of a single glance, is sublime—but it is also incredibly stupid, and so, in some respects, is Marius.

Book VII

Summary

In this book, Hugo introduces us to a number of Paris criminals; in particular, to Babet, Claquesous, Gueulemer, and Montparnasse, who governed the Paris underworld from 1830 to 1835. Gueulemer is a stupid strong man, thief, and murderer. Babet is a former tooth-puller who has also sold plaster busts and shown freaks at fairs; he is thin, supple, and absolutely without morals. Claquesous is a ventriloquist behind a mask; Montparnasse is young, good-looking, and ruthless.

Thanks to their various skills and their close relations, they have practically a monopoly of crime in the department of the Seine. With them work a number of other minor criminals, of whom Boulatruelle — the ex-convict we already met at Montfermeil — is one.

Commentary

In an epic description which perhaps may owe something to Dante's *Inferno*, Hugo now introduces us to the world that lies even below that of Les Misérables — the lowest depths of the criminal poor. The study of criminal life fascinated many nineteenth-century authors. Balzac has several novels in which the master criminal Vautrin appears; Dickens has his Fagin; and a number of popular French authors like Eugene Sué made adventures in the underworld their stock in trade.

Like most nineteenth-century reformers, Hugo is an environmentalist; that is, he believes that man is, on balance, naturally inclined to good, and that the evil in him is a product of his treatment by society. Crime, he says at the end of Chapter 2, will vanish with enlightenment. However, Hugo the writer is wiser than Hugo the theoretician; and in Book VIII he will invalidate everything he has said in Book VII by showing us a man whose criminality is not the result of his environment, and who is villainous as naturally as he breathes.

Book VIII

Summary

Summer passes, then fall. Winter comes. Neither M. Leblanc nor the young girl have reappeared at the Luxembourg Gardens. Marius is overwhelmed by an immense despair and a profound listlessness. One day he goes to a dance hall with the vague hope of encountering his lost love. The inevitable disappointment leaves him more depressed than ever, weary of people, obsessed with his anguish. Another day he has a strange encounter. He meets a man with long white hair who much resembles M. Leblanc but who is dressed as a workingman. Perplexed, Marius decides to investigate the mystery. But the passerby disappears before he can follow him.

On February 2, Marius witnesses a depressing scene that seems to be in keeping with his somber mood. He is passed by two girls, emaciated, ragged, barefoot. They are running, and from a word or two he overhears, Marius gathers that they are fleeing from the police. In her haste one of them drops an envelope and Marius picks it up. Before he can call them, they are out of earshot. He puts the envelope in his pocket and forgets it.

Undressing in the evening, he comes upon the envelope and examines it. In it he finds four letters addressed to prominent people, containing pleas for money and signed with the names of four different petitioners. But certain signs indicate the same author wrote all four. The handwriting, the paper, a peculiar tobacco odor, the spelling mistakes, are all identical. However, none of the letters bears an address, so Marius dismisses the mystery from his mind.

The next day as he is working, someone knocks on his door, and a young girl enters. She is no more than fifteen, but misery has already made her haggard. She gives Marius a letter from her father, Jondrette, asking for money. The face of the girl is not absolutely unknown to Marius. He seems to remember that he has seen her somewhere before. She calls Marius by name. He could not doubt that she means him, but who is this girl? How does she know his name? Even though Marius has been living in the house for some time, he has had, as we have said, very few occasions to observe his squalid neighborhood. His mind has been elsewhere, and where the mind is, there also are the eyes.

The letter from Jondrette is in the same handwriting as those in the packet Marius had picked up the day before. While Marius ponders the coincidence, the young girl frolics boldly around the room, sings, examines Marius' possessions, looks in the mirror. Finally, she tells him how handsome he is and accompanies her compliment with a meaningful look. Ignoring the hint, Marius hands her the package she has lost. Her manner changes; she is incredibly grateful and pours out to him a tale of constant hunger, suffering, hallucinations, and suicidal thoughts. Touched, Marius gives her his last five francs, and she thanks him in a flood of revolting but pathetic slang.

When she has left, Marius reflects on the depths of misery and degradation to which society allows a human being to sink. As he muses, he notices a triangular hole near the ceiling in the wall that divides his room from the Jondrettes'. Compassion is a spur to his curiosity, and he climbs on a dresser to observe his wretched neighbors. What he sees is a den: "abject, dirty, fetid, infected, dark, sordid." At a table sits a fairly old man who resembles both a shady businessman and a bird of prey. He is in the process of writing another begging letter and ranting against the injustices of life. Near the chimney sits his wife, a virago of indeterminate age. A listless, wan girl – the second fugitive of the day before – is resting on an old mattress.

Marius is about to leave his observation post when the older daughter walks in. She announces the imminent arrival of a potential benefactor, whom she has accosted during one of his frequent visits to St. Jacques Church. The father springs into action and orders various actions taken to worsen the squalid appearance of the room. He tells his wife to put out the fire, the younger daughter to break the seat of a chair, the eldest to break a window. The room is suitably devastated when the philanthropist walks in.

His entrance causes Marius an incredible shock. It is "M. Leblanc" and he is accompanied by his daughter, who is as lovely as ever. Meanwhile Jondrette, posing for this occasion as Fabantou, an actor down on his luck, launches into an emotional lament. As he details his real and pretended misfortunes, he stares hard at the visitor, as if trying to remember a familiar face. The latter, moved by the evident misery of the family, hands Jondrette five francs and a package of clothing, and promises to return at 6 P.M. with money for his rent.

Marius is an indifferent eyewitness to the whole scene. His only interest is the young girl. A moment after she leaves he runs after her. He reaches the street just in time to see her depart in a cab. He hails another, but since he has no money on him, the driver refuses to take him. In despair he turns back to his room. As he is about to climb the stairs he notices Jondrette in deep conversation with a man of menacing appearance. It is one of the most notorious hoodlums in the neighborhood.

As he mournfully enters his room, he is followed by Jondrette's older daughter. Marius is piqued at her, since by giving her his last five francs he has lost the opportunity to follow his elusive sweetheart. His resentment is particularly unfair, for the young girl's visit is motivated only by compassion and gratitude. She has noticed Marius' depressed air and is offering her help. Marius asks her to discover M. Leblanc's address. The young girl agrees, although with a sadness that Marius does not notice.

Alone again, Marius plunges into a poignant reverie. He is disturbed by Jondrette's excited comments about M. Leblanc and his daughter. Hoping to obtain some vital information, he jumps back on his observation post. He learns that Jondrette has recognized in M. Leblanc an old acquaintance, although obviously not a friend, since his wife greets the news with venomous rage. Jondrette, however, is pleased by the discovery, since he thinks he will be able to extort vast amounts of money from this old man. He has evidently hatched a sinister plot, judging from the ominous instructions to make up a fire which he gives his wife. Then he leaves to further perfect his trap.

Marius quickly resolves to checkmate whatever mischief Jondrette is planning. After a brief hesitation, he quietly sets out for the police station. On the way he overhears a conversation between two disreputable characters which confirms his suspicion that a net is closing around M. Leblanc. At the police station he is met by an inspector of impressive height with a piercing gaze. The interrogation is incisive and to the point. After his briefing, the policeman requests Marius' passkey and tells him to return home immediately. He is to observe the execution of the plot and, when the trap is about to be sprung, to shoot in the air as a signal to the police. As Marius leaves, as an afterthought the inspector gives him his name: Javert.

A little later Courfeyrac and Bossuet, Marius' student friends, run into him on the street. But he is unaware of their presence, as he is intently following Jondrette. The latter, not suspecting he is being followed, enters a hardware store and comes out with a chisel. Then he disappears into the shop of a man who hires out carriages. Marius gives up his spying to return home before the house is locked up for the night. On his way to his room he glimpses four men lurking in one of the empty apartments. But fearing to be seen, he refrains from investigating.

In his room he hears Jondrette returning, then giving various instructions and sending the two girls into the street as lookouts. He climbs back on the dresser and peers through the hole. The room is illuminated by an eerie red glow produced by a sizable stove full of burning coal, with a chisel in the middle of the fire. In a corner he notices two piles, one of old pieces of iron, the other of rope, which upon close examination turns out to be a ladder. Jondrette places two chairs at a table, lights his pipe, and waits.

The church bells strike six and, as agreed, M. Leblanc comes in. His first act is to hand Jondrette more money for his rent and his immediate needs. While he thanks him profusely, Jondrette manages to give his wife a disquieting order, "Send away the cab." Jondrette and Leblanc sit down and Jondrette holds his attention with talk while, unobtrusively, a man enters the room behind the old man's back.

Warned by a kind of instinct, M. Leblanc turns and perceives the new arrival. Jondrette explains him away as a neighbor, and the same explanation covers the arrival of three more sinister figures.

Then he explodes his bombshell: "Do you have your wallet? I'll settle for a thousand crowns." Leblanc, alarmed by this blackmail, stands up with his back to the wall and stares at him suspiciously. Like a cat playing with a mouse, Jondrette turns to more innocent conversation. Suddenly three armed men walk in and Jondrette ceases his pretense. In a thunderous voice he says to Leblanc: "Do you recognize me?" Leblanc, pale but far from intimidated, retreats behind the table and steels himself for action, declaring he does not know Jondrette. Jondrette cries, "I am not Fabantou. I am not Jondrette. I am Thénardier."

The revelation leaves Leblanc unmoved, but not Marius. He is stunned, for he finds himself confronted by an impossible dilemma: save Thénardier and sacrifice an innocent man or call the police and betray his father's trust. He has no time to deliberate, for events move rapidly. Thénardier savors his triumph with hysterical glee, pouring out a flood of reproaches, threats and boasts; Leblanc calmly replies that Thénardier is mistaken, he is not a rich man, and they have never met before. But, as Thénardier turns around to speak to one of his accomplices, the prisoner springs to the window and nearly escapes. It takes three men to bring him back and, after a titanic struggle, he is tied to one of the beds.

Thénardier then sends the gang out and tries another tactic. Shrewdly he points out to Leblanc that in spite of his danger he has never called for help. Can it be that he is afraid of the police? With elaborate casualness, he moves to give the old man a view of the red-hot chisel; and proposes a bargain — 200,000 francs for Leblanc's freedom. With the smile of a "grand inquisitor," he invites Leblanc to write a letter to his daughter asking her to come to him; she will serve as a hostage to insure that Leblanc pays the money. Silently, Leblanc writes, signs his name, and gives his address. Convulsively, Thénardier grasps the letter and sends his wife out with it to get the girl. They wait in a long and dreadful silence until Mme. Thénardier returns in a fury. They have been duped: Leblanc has given them a false address.

While she has been gone, however, Leblanc has used a miniature saw hidden in a hollow coin in his pocket to cut his bonds, and he is free except for one leg. He leaps to his feet and defies them, seizing the red-hot chisel in one hand. "You will never make me write what I do not want to write," he cries, and disdainfully puts the chisel to his own arm, watching it burn without a quiver; then he flings the chisel out of the window. The gang falls upon him, and Thénardier, deciding there is nothing left to do but kill him, takes a knife from the drawer.

Marius is in an agony of indecision, but he can no longer delay—it is Leblanc or Thénardier. Suddenly he has an inspiration; During her visit that morning. Thénardier's daughter had written on a piece of paper to show her education, "The cops are here." Marius grabs it and throws it through the crack in the wall. The gang reacts just as he has hoped. They rush to the window in a disorderly panic.

But their escape is foiled by Javert's dramatic appearance. His authority reduces them to a flock of sheep. Thénardier alone among the men offers some resistance; he aims a pistol at Javert, but the gun misfires. In bestial fury, his wife hurls a rock at the inspector, who simply ducks. The police put handcuffs on the gang, and the three masked men are identified: they are Gueulemer, Babet, and Claquesous, three of the four bandit chiefs of Paris. His prisoners secured, Javert looks around for the victim, but in the confusion he has vanished. "The devil!" says Javert. "He must have been the best catch of the lot."

The next day Gavroche goes to see his parents, impertinent and carefree as usual. He finds the door to their apartment closed, and an old lady whom he has just insulted informs him that his whole family is in jail. He greets the news with a casual, "Ah!" and with a song on his lips returns to the wintry street.

Commentary

Hugo has an instinct for innocence; with sexually mature women characters he is sometimes uneasy as a writer, but with the girl-woman his touch is unerring. Confronted by the elder Jondrette girl, with her torn bodice, her harsh voice, and her abominable argot, he looks beyond the surface and shows us hunger, grief, modesty, shame, courage, a longing for affection and even for respectability. Through her and her sister, he gives us a vivid illustration of his thesis that "le misère de l'enfant" is the most appalling of all.

However, this is not his only purpose in introducing them. Where his plot is concerned, he is taking up again, on a deeper, more human level, the Cinderella theme treated at the beginning of Book II. These two creatures in rags were once the spoiled darlings, Eponine and Azelma; the "ugly sisters" have become ugly indeed, and when Cosette appears before her erstwhile tormentors in silk cloak and velvet hat she takes a crushing revenge, though she is quite unaware of it. The irony of their meeting is mingled with tragedy: Eponine and Azelma were, at Montfermeil, and are still, only children and no more deserve their present fate than Cosette deserved her ill-treatment at the inn. All three have been equally victims of Thénardier.

Thénardier is the most enigmatic of the characters in *Les Misérables*, and during most of Book VIII he has us, like Marius, standing on tiptoe with an eye to the peephole to see what he will do next.

"Evil" is not an exact adjective for Thénardier, nor is "criminal," though he is both. "Perverse" describes him more precisely; he is incurably perverse, and his perversity ruins his own life as well as that of others. He is not without intelligence and education, and when we saw him last he was proprietor of his own inn, with 1,550 francs of debts, of which Jean Valjean had just relieved him by buying Cosette. There was no reason why he could not have led a reasonably prosperous life. However, even then, far from being content with his luck, he followed Jean Valjean to extort more funds and was nearly killed by the goose that laid the golden egg. As Jondrette, he behaves in exactly the same way: in the hope of one extra franc of charity, he destroys two francs' worth of chair, window, and fire — not to speak of injuring Azelma; and when he is assured of regular help from Valjean-Leblanc, he throws it away in the vain hope of wringing his whole fortune from the ex-convict. Never satisfied with what he has, each failure leaves him poorer and more embittered.

The most dangerous thing about him, however, is the power of his fantasy to obscure the truth. When he tells Valjean in Part Two how fond he is of Cosette, how much he will miss her, we have to think twice to reestablish the real facts; and when he rails against society in the garret, he almost convinces us that it is the world and not himself who is responsible for all his troubles. In his presence, even Jean Valjean's image becomes distorted, and from behind the facade of the philanthropist emerges again the figure of the convict, complete with prison ruses, secret escape coin, and superhuman strength. As for Marius, Thénardier's old lie on the field of Waterloo has him so confused he does not know whether or how to come to Jean Valjean's aid. This, however, is the least of Marius' unwitting sins against Cosette's foster-father; by notifying the police, he has put Javert back on Jean Valjean's track again.

The "recognition scene," in which one character turns out to be other than he appears, has been a common device for achieving dramatic surprise since the Greeks; with the superb nonchalance of a great writer, Hugo tops off Part Three with a quintuple recognition scene. We have, of course, suspected for a long time that the Jondrettes are really the Thénardiers, but the confirmation is satisfying; and there is even some genuine surprise in our realization that Gavroche is the baby we heard wailing, neglected, at the inn when Jean Valjean came to find Cosette.

Les Misérables is, like a drama, divided into five sections, and its inner structure parallels that of a drama as well. The first act is a highly suspenseful exposition; the second one—as all too often on the stage, unfortunately, drags; the fourth and fifth are reserved for climax and denouement. At the end of the third act, most dramatists like to provide a subclimax, only slightly less powerful than that at the end of the fourth. This is the pattern of most of Shakespeare's tragedies, and it is the pattern Hugo follows here, bringing together, at almost exactly the midpoint of the book, all his key characters in a dramatic confrontation. The confrontation is, however, inconclusive for all of them and we are left in the expectation of a more decisive encounter later on.

PART FOUR: ST. DENIS

Book I

Summary

Hugo interrupts his narrative to give a historical sketch of the background and beginning of the July Monarchy, which was established by the Revolution of 1830. After Napoleon fell, he was followed by the two Bourbon kings Louis XVIII and Charles X, who reigned from 1814 to 1830. This period was known as the Restoration, and it was marked by a great longing for peace, a great weariness after the heroic days of the Republic and the Empire. However, the people were not so passive that they did not demand the retention of the freedoms won by the Revolution. These the Bourbons grudgingly granted, but they acted in bad faith. When, in 1830, Charles X felt himself sufficiently strong to do so, he attempted to abrogate his concessions. It was a grievous miscalculation. The nation rebelled and the king was deposed and exiled.

Unfortunately, the revolution was captured by opportunists. Pleading the need for peace and order, they restored the monarchy. Their choice fell upon Louis Philippe, a representative of the Orléans, the younger branch of the royal family. While the move was designed to protect the privileges of the bourgeoisie against the people, it was, however, not a complete retrogression. It confirmed certain democratic gains, though it stopped short of giving the people full sovereignty.

The hybrid character of the revolution is illustrated by the king it selected. Louis Philippe, nicknamed Egalité (equality), was, in spite of his royal ancestry, sympathetic to liberal ideas. Unlike his predecessors, he had been on the side of the people during the events of 1789 and had even participated actively in them. During his reign, he not only respected the prerogatives of his subjects but actively concerned himself with their welfare. He frequently intervened, for instance, in favor of political prisoners. Nevertheless the beginning of the king's reign was not auspicious. On the one hand, Louis Philippe was attacked by the conservatives who could not resign themselves to the loss of their privileges. On the other, he was not acceptable to the republicans, for whom any monarchy, however enlightened, was a betrayal of their ideal.

Behind the visible resistance, a quieter, more pervasive opposition was growing to the whole concept of monarchy and government by the propertied classes. Socialist thinkers were critically reexamining the whole structure of society and undermining its old foundations. Thus, two years after the overthrow of the Bourbons, radical ideas, international tensions, and popular discontent already were forming heavy clouds on the political horizon. In April, 1832, the situation has become explosive. The Saint Antoine section, the most volatile in Paris, is openly planning revolution. Discussion groups examine the legitimacy of the government; militants gird for action. Extremists manufacture bullets, and the police report that a veritable arsenal is being collected.

Inevitably, the revolutionary fever spreads. Secret societies, increasingly defiant, proliferate and spread like a cancer through the body politic. First Paris is infected, then the provinces. Marius' old friends take an active part in the seditious activities. A.B.C. leader Enjolras dispatches his lieutenants to various groups of students and workers to organize them for the revolution. Enjolras reserves for himself the group known as La Cougourde. On his way to meet them, he mulls over the situation and optimistically foresees a glorious uprising leading to the ultimate emancipation of the people.

A slight disappointment, however, mars his grandiose vision. In passing he decides to inspect the work of his friend Grantaire, the cynic who has only become a revolutionary out of admiration for

Enjolras. Instead of haranguing the workers whose revolutionary fervor he was supposed to excite, Grantaire is engaged in an absorbing game of dominoes with them.

Commentary

Hugo's long discussion of the political evolution of France from 1815 to 1832 is primarily a republican political document. It is intended to hearten French republicans by reminding them that, despite many checks, republicanism has steadily gained ground in the nineteenth century and to encourage his readers to oppose the Empire, which subverted the Republic of 1848. And as usual, Hugo, the political exile, is a very effective propagandist. The book, however, also serves as an introduction to the revolt of 1832, which will involve most of the characters we have met so far in *Les Misérables;* and the activity of Enjolras and his group foreshadows this important plot development.

Books II-III

Summary

After Thénardier's arrest, Marius immediately leaves his room and moves in with Courfeyrac, who receives him with the simple hospitality of a true friend. Marius has two reasons for the move. First, the viciousness he has witnessed makes him loathe the Gorbeau tenement; and second, he does not want to testify against Thénardier. As the months go by, Marius sinks back into a state of depression. The happiness that he has glimpsed has again vanished. This time the loss of his beloved seems irreparable; he cannot find even the most tenuous link with her. He is disturbed, also, by her "father's" equivocal behavior. The old gentleman's refusal to call for help, his quiet escape, are highly suspicious.

Material difficulties compound his misery. Once again Marius is plagued by poverty. Too discouraged to work, he has quit his job and abandons himself to a dangerous reverie that increases his lethargy. Absorbed by the vision of his lost love, he contemplates impassively his inexorable disintegration. Unfit for practical activities, he is only capable of absurd and romantic gestures. In a notebook he writes ethereal love letters destined never to be read. Because the Thénardiers called the girl he loves "the Lark," her Montfermeil nickname, he makes regular pilgrimages to an isolated area called "the Field of the Lark."

Hugo now takes us to visit Javert, who is not happy. Thénardier's prisoner, who would probably have been an interesting prize for the police, has vanished, and two of the gangsters — Montparnasse and Claquesous — have slipped between his fingers too. The latter's escape is particularly humiliating, since it was engineered in the police vehicle itself. The rest of the gang are also far from inactive. One of its imprisoned members, Brujon, is engaging in suspicious maneuvers. He dispatches three messages to confederates on the outside. One day a guard catches him in the act of writing a letter, but the letter disappears before the guard can seize it.

The next day a note wrapped in a ball of bread reaches Babet, one of the leaders of the Patron-Minette gang. From Babet, it goes to Eponine, who inspects the house in the Rue Plumet. As an answer Eponine returns a biscuit, which in the mysterious code of the underworld means "nothing doing." This abortive criminal plot has totally unexpected consequences. It acquaints Eponine with Cosette's whereabouts, and this piece of information soon changes the latter's destiny and that of her lover Marius.

Marius' old friend Mabeuf, the churchwarden, has been suffering a decline which resembles that of Marius himself. His major source of income, his book *Flora of Cauteretz,* is not selling at all. His experiments on indigo are a failure. His breakfast is reduced to two eggs, and often it is his only meal. One peaceful evening, Mabeuf sees a strange apparition. Exhausted from his day's work on his indigo experiments, he rests in his garden with a book in his hands while he anxiously studies his magnificent rhododendron, threatened by drought. He would like to water his flowers, but he doesn't even have the strength to unhook the chain from the well. Unexpectedly, he has a bizarre visitor, a ragged, undernourished girl who proceeds to water his whole garden for him. As a reward she asks for Marius' address and disappears as soon as she has learned it.

A few days later Marius, restless and unable to work, has gone on his usual pilgrimage to the Field of the Lark. Sadly he is thinking of "her," and his sadness is aggravated by self-reproach. His reverie is broken by Eponine's appearance. She addresses him in a babbling mixture of delight, naive questions, explanations, and compassion. The girl is obviously and pathetically in love with him. At last, since he shows no interest in her as a person, she tells him that she knows Cosette's address. Marius is ecstatic and, blinded by love, ignores the tragic effect his happiness has on Eponine. He is concerned only with his sweetheart's safety and makes Eponine promise she will not reveal the address to her father. She reminds him that he has promised her a reward, and he gives her five francs. Somberly she drops it with the comment, "I don't want your money."

In the suburb of Saint Germain is located an unobtrusive little house, the former love nest of an eighteenth-century magistrate. Among its features, there is a secret exit onto another street which allowed the amorous but prudent judge to visit his mistress without arousing suspicion. In October, 1829, Jean Valjean has rented the long-vacant house under the name of Fauchelevent, reopened the secret passageway, and installed Cosette and an old servant, Toussaint, in this new residence. In spite of his happiness in the convent he decided after much thought to leave Little Picpus. He felt that he owed it to Cosette to provide her with a normal life in spite of the dangers this would present to his personal safety. As an added precaution, he has rented two other old apartments in Paris as potential retreats; one is that to which Marius previously traced Cosette.

Except for a few luxuries for Cosette the pair lives modestly and above all discreetly. They take walks in the Luxembourg Gardens, go to mass, give generously to the beggars at the door of the church, and visit the poor and sick. Valjean serves in the National Guard, an obligation that he welcomes, since it gives him an aura of respectability. Buoyed by Cosette's companionship, Valjean enjoys the simplicity of his new life.

The young girl is happy too. Her garden is a world of endless discoveries. In Valjean she finds an interesting friend who shares with her the fruits of his wide readings; he is her universe, both father and mother to her, and she fusses over his cold room and his Spartan diet. She hardly remembers her past and has completely forgotten her mother, for Valjean never mentions her. A mysterious instinct warns her that her origins are a subject better left unmentioned.

But unsuspected dangers threaten their tranquility. Cosette is about to enter adolescence, an age of temptations and longings for which she is completely unprepared. Her ignorance, carefully protected by the convent, only enhances the intensity of desires that she experiences without understanding. Valjean, a bachelor quite unused to women, is unable to help her.

One day Cosette suddenly realizes that she is very pretty. What her mirror has hinted is confirmed by the comments of a passerby and the observations of the old servant Toussaint. With inexpressible satisfaction she realizes that her skin is a satiny white, her hair lustrous and beautiful, her blue eyes splendid. Valjean, however, is dismayed by her beauty; he is dimly aware that any change threatens his happiness and that another may some day steal Cosette from him. Nevertheless, he does not prevent her from ordering an elegant new wardrobe nor from parading her gracefulness in public.

It is at this time that Cosette meets Marius in the park. Subconsciously she notes his good looks, his air of intelligence, his gentleness. Then their eyes meet, and his glance produces the same effect on her as hers on him. Love, in turn, unleashes a multitude of incomprehensible and contradictory emotions in her. At first she is angry at Marius' apparent indifference, then she boldly approaches him in the park. Later melancholy overtakes her, and she suffers the traditional sleeplessness, agitation, and fever. Still her love remains distant, "a mute contemplation, the deification of a stranger."

Valjean, too, is aware of Marius. Unlike Cosette, he views him as a threat and lays traps for him. He changes benches, drops his handkerchief, comes alone to the park. When Marius' reactions betray his interest in Cosette, Valjean grows hateful and ferocious and watches him like "a hound looking at a thief." When Marius makes the mistake of questioning the doorman, Valjean moves to the Rue Plumet without leaving a trace. Cosette accepts her fate without complaint; indeed, she has no vocabulary to express any of the feelings she now experiences. But she falls into a profound despondency which becomes deeper as the separation from Marius lengthens. Valjean notices her sadness and is heartbroken, but he does not know how to cure it. Tragically, Cosette and her foster father come to hurt each other deeply in spite of their mutual love.

One morning a somber incident deepens their gloom. As is their wont, they are taking a walk to enjoy the glory of sunrise. For a moment they are consoled by the serenity of the hour. Then a harsh noise disturbs their peace: it is the forerunner of a dreary spectacle, a long convoy of prisoners. A mass of convicts, sinister and dehumanized, are being transported to the galleys on seven tumbrils escorted by rows of equally sinister guards. The scene is one of degradation, brutality, misery, and filth. Valjean is pertrified by this vision from his past, and the sensitive Cosette is equally frightened.

Commentary

In these two books, through many rapid changes of scene, Hugo is maneuvering all his characters toward a crisis and preparing also for the denouement of the love story in the next part. Five of his characters — Marius, M. Mabeut, Eponine, Cosette, and Jean Valjean — are undergoing a period of sorrow and doubt. For Marius, this period of inactivity and passivity is a prelude to a violent reaction which will once more reunite him with the realities of life and decide his destiny for good or ill. The despair of Eponine and M. Mabeuf, which has more valid causes, will also produce dramatic decisions and drastic consequences. Cosette's unhappiness deepens and strengthens her feeling for Marius, and by learning to bear sorrow with patience, she matures from girl into woman. As for Jean Valjean, his anger and grief are a normal response to the foreknowledge that yet one more sacrifice will soon be demanded of him, and this the greatest sacrifice of all.

Skillfully, Hugo uses Eponine not only to win our sympathy but to further plot and character development. A waif just out of prison, she is a figure pathetic enough to cause any bourgeois to subscribe promptly to public education and child welfare, but she also serves as a link between the criminals, Marius, M. Mabeuf, and Cosette and Jean. Finally, her love for Marius, which Marius ignores, points up the egoism of his blind devotion to his unknown love — a devotion that has already made him idle and neglectful of his own future. Marius, young hero though he is, is far from perfect — perfection is a privilege that will ultimately be reserved for the elderly Jean Valjean.

Jean Valjean, however, is right to fear him, just because he is young and in love and because nature is therefore on his side. Good parenthood always ends in a painful separation because it is a parent's function to prepare the child to leave home and become a good parent in his turn. Jean Valjean has courageously taken the first step in this direction already by taking Cosette out of the convent and allowing her the liberty to choose what her future life will be. Nature, in making her beautiful, takes the next step; Marius is simply the inevitable conclusion of a normal series of developments.

The garden of the Rue Plumet is the image of Cosette's spirit — innocent, beautiful, and wild — and Jean Valjean has until now been privileged to share its springtime joy. Cosette's true companion, however, is on his way, and once he arrives Jean Valjean will again be shut out in the shadows of his past, as the scene with the convicts at the Barrière du Maine implies.

Summary

During the period when both he and Cosette are unhappy, Valjean makes his historic visit to the Thénardiers. When he comes back the next day with an ugly wound on his arm that keeps him in bed with a fever for a month, Cosette cares for him with angelic devotion. Their renewed intimacy fills Jean Valjean with delight and Cosette, for her part, finds a distraction in her new responsibilities and satisfaction in her father's improvement. Then April comes, and spring is an infallible balm for a young and delicate soul.

One evening Gavroche, tired of a two-day fast, decides to go on a food-hunting expedition. In investigating an apple bin in a garden, he overhears a conversation between M. Mabeuf and his old servant, Mother Plutarch. She is reminding him there is no food in the larder, and no one will give them credit because they owe money everywhere.

This doleful exchange compels Gavroche to abandon his designs on the apple bin and to think about this poverty even greater than his own. He is distracted from his meditations by a puzzling and alarming sight. An old gentleman is strolling toward him, unaware that he is being followed by Montparnasse, Gavroche's underworld friend. Before the urchin has a chance to intervene, the thief pounces on his intended victim. But he has underestimated his opponent. To his immense humiliation, he is beaten to the ground and held as if by a vise. Without letting go, the passerby gives him a sobering lecture, a preview of his potential fate as a convict in a living hell. Then he hands Montparnasse his purse and quietly resumes his walk. Montparnasse is stunned — a fatal paralysis. Gavroche sneaks up on him like a cat, steals his purse, and drops it in Mabeuf's garden. Mabeuf cannot believe his eyes as the purse falls from the sky before him.

Cosette continues to recover from her heartbreak. She seems to have forgotten Marius, and begins to take an interest in a handsome young officer who struts daily in front of her garden, and who is really Théodule, a grandnephew of M. Gillenormand. Cosette has more resiliency than Marius, who seems to be trapped in his dream of love.

One evening during one of Valjean's periodic absences Cosette has a disquieting experience. She hears what sounds like a man's footsteps in the garden. The next evening she hears the same footsteps and then sees a shadow, a terrifying shadow topped by a man's hat. By the time she turns around, the shadow has disappeared. When Valjean comes back she tells him of her alarms. He, deeply preoccupied, spends the next three nights in the garden. The third night he calls her down to show her the explanation of the mystery: the shadow of a nearby chimney which might easily be mistaken for that of a man.

A few days later, however, a new incident occurs. Cosette is sitting, in the melancholy of nightfall, on a bench near the garden gate. Slowly she gets up, strolls through the garden, and returns to her seat. On the spot she just vacated on the bench there now lies a stone. This time she is genuinely frightened, all the more so since her father has gone on one of his nocturnal walks. Feverishly she runs inside, barricades the house, and spends a restless night.

In the morning, the sun dissipates her apprehension and she dismisses the incident as a nightmare. But when she returns to the garden she finds that the stone is real. Fright gives way to curiosity and she examines the stone more closely. Under it she discovers a notebook containing a kind of prose poem celebrating the splendors of love. Cosette intuitively recognizes the author of the letter and simultaneously the truth about her own emotions. Her love for Marius had become an ember, but never died. Now it blazes up again to a bright new flame. At that moment the handsome lieutenant passes by and Cosette finds him supremely unpleasing.

During her evening stroll in the garden she has the sudden feeling of a presence behind her. She turns her head and sees Marius, gaunt and spectral. She is overwhelmed by his humble, poignant declaration of love and reciprocates with her own. They kiss and are transported out of this world. After a long moment of silent ecstasy, they proceed to mutual confessions of their deepest feelings. Two souls melt into one. Only after their reunion is complete do they ask each other their names.

Commentary

In character portrayal, Hugo prefers to reveal personality through simple feeling and direct action, and seldom indulges in the lengthy and complex psychological analysis of such later nineteenth-century writers as Marcel Proust. Jean Valjean's lecture to Montparnasse on laziness is one of his rare excursions into abstract psychology, and it is a remarkable one. Hugo, like the medieval church, recognizes that sloth, as opposed to occasional holiday idleness, is a mortal sin. Man's only lasting happiness lies in work, and the refusal to work leads to the total destruction of the personality. The passage is interesting, too, because it is one of the rare occasions on which Hugo gives us an insight into Jean Valjean's thinking. Indeed, Valjean cannot properly be said to think; rather, he turns things over and over in his mind until a conclusion evolves, and the conclusion is usually remarkably wise.

The reunion of Marius and Cosette is unquestionably one of the most touching scenes in literature despite, or perhaps because of, the touch of humor with which Hugo introduces it. While Marius is dying for love, Cosette has almost forgotten him—but not for long. With superb suspense, Hugo brings him closer and closer to her, as a sound of footsteps, a shadow, a letter, and finally Marius himself. Nor does Hugo spare any of the resources of his art to enhance the drama of their meeting and mutual avowals. The essence of his poetry has gone into Marius' love letter; the garden in springtime offers the perfect setting for first love; and Cosette's poignant cry, "O ma mère!" seems to set the seal of heaven itself on their union.

Book VI

Summary

After 1823, the Thénardiers had two more sons whom the mother hated and managed to get rid of in a very efficient way. A friend, Magnon—the woman who had persuaded M. Gillenormand to support them—lost her two illegitimate sons in an epidemic. In order to conserve her income she needed replacements; and these Mme. Thénardier provided, to their mutual convenience. The children benefit temporarily from the exchange. Magnon treats them kindly because of the money they represent. But she is implicated in the Thénardier affair and arrested. The children are left to wander alone in the streets of Paris.

One cold spring day of 1832 Gavroche is standing in front of the window of a barbershop. He is waiting for a propitious moment to steal a cake of soap which he hopes to sell in the suburbs. While Gavroche is preparing his bit of larceny, two little boys enter the shop to ask for help and are harshly rebuffed. Touched by their tears, the urchin takes them royally in tow, and leads them in the rain to a baker's, where he manages to extract a small coin from his pocket and buy them and himself a piece of bread. On the way he has passed a girl in rags and given her the woman's shawl he wears for warmth over his shoulders.

After their casual meal, the boys and Gavroche resume their walk until they meet Montparnasse, wearing dark glasses. Their conversation is brief, inhibited by the arrival of a policeman. At last the waifs reach the Place de la Bastille, where Gavroche has a unique domicile, the inside of the statue of an elephant which has been neglected by the authorities. Gavroche shows the children how to get in by climbing one of the elephant's legs and entering through a hole in his belly. The older boy follows Gavroche and the younger one, more timid, is carried up the ladder.

Once inside, Gavroche closes the hole and lights a candle. He comforts the frightened children with a mixture of gruffness and solicitude. Then he shows them his bedroom, a kind of cage made of metal trellis to protect him against the army of rats who share his quarters. At the thought of rats, the children begin to cry again, so he cheers them by painting a picture of all the delights he has in store for them — shows, swimming, and mischief. After he blows out the candle, the older boy falls asleep; but his brother is still terrified of the rats, which are excited by the presence of human flesh. Gavroche gives him a reassuring hand and soon all three are asleep, oblivious to the harsh world outside.

At dawn, Gavroche is awakened by Montparnasse. The latter needs his help and Gavroche follows him without a question. They go to La Force prison to help Brujon, Thénardier, and Gueulemer, who are planing an escape.

With a providential nail, Brujon has that night managed to make a hole in a chimney, and with Gueulemer he has climbed to the roof. Then they lower themselves with a rope they have brought along. A few minutes later they join Montparnasse and Babet, who has escaped some time before.

Now it is Thénardier's turn. He drugs his guard with doped wine and with a metal pin breaks his chains. But he is not out of danger yet. His friends have left him a piece of rope too short to reach the ground and he must seek a different avenue of escape. With the mysterious instinct of despair he finds his way to the roof of a building outside the prison walls. But his prodigious effort is futile: he is too weak and the ground is too far below for him to climb down the facade of the building. Suddenly he notices his confederates below debating whether or not they should give him up and leave. Afraid to speak, he signals by throwing them his hitherto useless piece of rope.

At the instigation of the others, Gavroche with careless courage climbs a rickety pipe to the roof and carries his father another, longer rope. No sooner has Thénardier reached freedom than he and the rest of the gang begin to discuss a subject that had earlier been debated in prison: a possible coup against Valjean, Rue Plumet. Then they disband, and as Thénardier departs Babet says to him, "Did you notice the boy who brought you the rope? I think he was your son." "Bah," says Thénardier, "do you think so?" and the subject is forgotten.

Commentary

Gavroche provides us with an excellent example of Hugo's technique in character development. Hugo introduces him to us first simply as a member of a species, the Paris gamin, and gives us to understand that he possesses the courage, impertinence, and ingenuity of his kind, but he says little about Gavroche as an individual. He remains for us only the silhouette of a boy with his hands in his pockets who passes us in the street whistling. In Part Four, however, Hugo begins to fill in this outline with precise details of speech and behavior. Gavroche wears a woman's shawl and gives it away on a cold day; he steals soap and buys little boys bread; he helps criminals escape, but steals from them to help poor old men; and he lives in an elephant. He becomes a contradictory, colorful, lively personality, totally unlike anyone but himself.

But this realistic character study also carries social and spiritual overtones. The picture of Gavroche aiding his little brothers and his father, quite unaware of their relationship to him, underlines a social tragedy — the disintegration of the family under the pressures of poverty. And his comment on his two little lost wards, "All the same, If I had children, I would take better care of them that that," is a masterpiece of dramatic and social irony. This waif of the streets, to whom society has never given any material help or moral training, has a far deeper compassion for childhood, and a far sharper sense of his moral responsibility toward the unprotected, than an average adult French citizen like the barber.

Gavroche is also, however, a spiritual symbol. Without comment and without sentimentality, Hugo through him unfolds to us the natural simple Christianity of the gospels. With cheerful patience Gavroche makes fun of his own troubles, but he is keenly sensitive to the sufferings of others. Hungry, he feeds M. Mabeuf; cold, he clothes the shivering girl he meets on the street. Whatever he has, he shares with the poor;

he suffers little children to come unto him; he is kind to those who despitefully use him; and he even manages, against all odds, to honor his father and mother. Unlike Jean Valjean, who has to struggle with himself to achieve good, Gavroche comes by it naturally—even gaily; but neither is inferior to the other. Both are types of the Christian spirit triumphing over adversity.

Book VII

Summary

In Book VII, Hugo digresses to defend his use of slang. Slang, he concedes, is a horrible, pestilential language. But the novelist no more than the scientist can exclude any phenomenon from his field of inquiry, however unpalatable. Slang in its purest sense is the weapon of the have-nots against the establishment. Hence its preservation is of sociological interest. Furthermore, the study of slang is a means of curing the misfortune that has engendered it.

The spirit of slang, admittedly, is evil. "It is a dressing room in which the language disguises itself because it has some evil deed to do." But let us be merciful to it and to those who speak it, for human existence seems to indicate that none of us is free of guilt. The universal unhappiness of mankind seems to suggest that all of us are carrying the burden of divine retribution.

Slang, besides its ethical interest, has a literary value. It is the poetry of evil. It is a kind of geological formation whose numerous layers contain the fossils of various foreign words. It coins evocative expressions, it creates metaphors, it freely reshapes the language. Slang is dynamic, ever changing. It is the mirror of a soul, for a close study of it reveals the psychology of the underworld.

Commentary

Victor Hugo is not the only nineteenth-century novelist to immortalize slang in his pages. Zola, Balzac, Dickens—all frequently use slang and dialect in their novels to add authenticity and realism to the speech of their characters. This was, however, still considered an innovation, and not always a desirable one. Many people in the nineteenth century were still horrified to find such "vulgar" language in a work of art, so Book VII is really a document setting forth Hugo's views on a lively literary controversy.

In the sixteenth century, the poets of the French *Pléiade* introduced a number of new dialectal and technical words into the French literary vocabulary in order to make the French language more flexible and more representative of the wider world of the Renaissance. The classical writers of the seventeenth century, however, adopted the doctrine that true art dealt only with the noble and the beautiful, and expressed it in universal and general terms. In accordance with this view, they purified literary language of most of its colorful "special" terminology, and writers of the eighteenth century narrowed the vocabulary yet further to the point of monotony. The early Romantics, in their revolt against classical strictures on art, rebelled against restrictions on vocabulary too.

Hugo was one of the leaders of this movement, and almost single-handed brought about a complete revolution in the concept of "poetic" vocabulary. "I have put the red bonnet of the Revolution on the old dictionary," he said, and in language he used any word that pleased him — exotic, learned, archaic, technical, or vulgar — as long as it conveyed his meaning more effectively. Here, he defends slang because it seems to him a colorful expression of the poetry of the people, the authentic voice of their courage and their defiant despair. Today, thanks to Hugo and others like him, there are no censored words in literature, and writers have a freer artistic vocabulary than ever before.

Books VIII-IX

Summary

During the month of May, Marius visits Cosette every evening in the garden and they live an idyll of chaste adoration. They exchange trivial observations charged with emotion. They laugh lightheartedly. Marius pays Cosette admiring compliments and Cosette confesses her love. They simply enjoy the plenitude of existence. Valjean is completely unaware of Marius' visits. The young man comes when the old man has retired. Cosette is extremely amenable, never objecting to Valjean's plans and suggestions.

Unfortunately, complications are about to disturb the perfect simplicity of the couple's lives. One day Marius meets Eponine. Egoistic like all lovers, he has completely forgotten her. He finds the meeting awkward and she, for different reasons, is embarrassed too. They exchange only a few words. The next day Marius sees Eponine again. He avoids her, but she follows him to the Rue Plumet and hides in a dark corner outside the gate, lost in unhappy thoughts.

Soon after, six men meet in front of the house. It is Thénardier's gang, planning to carry out the robbery of Valjean's house which they had first discussed in prison. Eponine abruptly leaves her hiding place and, as a diversionary tactic, she embraces her father and greets his accomplices. When cajolery proves ineffective, she turns to defiance. Alone, this frail creature challenges the entire gang, and even when threatened with death, declares she will rouse the whole neighborhood at the first hostile move. Her firmness alarms the thieves, who reluctantly abandon their project and scatter in the night.

But misfortune, checked in one direction, attacks in another. While Eponine stands guard outside, Cosette gives Marius a piece of news that is the equivalent of a death sentence. Jean Valjean, alarmed by a sense that he is watched, has decided to take her to England. Confronted by this catastrophe, Marius makes a desperate resolution. He will go to see his grandfather and appeal to his pity. Had he seen M. Gillenormand recently, Marius might be more hopeful, for the old man has been undergoing a transformation. His self-righteousness has given place to sorrow and he thinks about Marius with more affection and less bitterness. The sudden realization that their separation may be permanent has cut him to the heart.

Marius' unexpected visit provokes an immense longing for reconciliation which, alas, the old man cannot express. He greets Marius with his usual severity and his grandson responds with constraint. Angry at himself for his inept behavior and at Marius for his obtuseness, he vehemently refuses him permission to marry. His answer is a long, bitter, sarcastic diatribe climaxed by an irrevocable: "Never!"

In his distress Marius cries out: "Father!" and this word proves the open sesame to the old man's heart. Abruptly he is transfigured, embraces Marius, seats him in an armchair, and listens with the deepest sympathy to his love story. But no amount of understanding can quite bridge the gap between the libertine eighteenth-century grandfather and the romantic nineteenth-century grandson. To the grandfather, Marius' love affair is only a youthful escapade, and he suggests that he make Cosette his mistress. Marius is deeply offended by this suggestion and leaves indignantly. M. Gillenormand, thunderstruck, believes that this time the rift is irreparable, and he sinks into an agony of grief that transcends tears.

Meanwhile Valjean, sitting on a slope in the Champ de Mars, is pondering the new dangers that are threatening his safety. Several times he has seen Thénardier roaming the neighborhood. The political unrest has made the police extremely vigilant, and he is afraid of becoming an accidental victim of their investigations. Finally, a fresh and enigmatic inscription on his garden wall adds to his preoccupation; "16 Rue de la Verrerie" is simply Marius' address, which he has written on the wall so that Cosette will know where to find him, but to Valjean it is a sinister sign. As he ponders, a note from the ever-watchful Eponine falls in front of him. It contains one significant word: "Move." This is the last straw; he decides to obey the note's warning.

Marius leaves his grandfather's house in a state of absolute despair. His rational faculties have abandoned him and, like a robot, he walks the streets for hours. The next day, after a restless night, he resumes his wanderings; but without really knowing why, he takes Javert's pistols with him. Obsessed by his pain and the thought of his last rendezvous with Cosette, he is only dimly aware of the rumblings of the uprising.

At nine o'clock in the evening he arrives at the garden to say goodbye to his love forever. But he is to be denied this last consolation. Jean Valjean has already taken Cosette away, and Marius falls on the bench like a man who has received a mortal blow. Then, through the trees, a dim figure whispers a message. "Monsieur Marius, your friends are waiting for you at the barricade in the Rue de la Chanvrerie."

M. Mabeuf is also in despair. He has been sinking to the last stages of destitution. Gavroche's purse has done him no good, since in his naive honesty he has taken it to the police. His indigo experiment has been a total failure. The plates of his books have been sold to a pawnbroker. He cannot even afford his starvation diet, and he has been forced to the supreme sacrifice of selling his rare books. The promised help of a cabinet member proves a disappointment. At last he is reduced to disposing of his most precious volume, a book by Diogenes Laertius, to buy medicine for his sick servant. When he hears shots in the direction of the Arsenal, he takes his hat and goes out.

Commentary

Skillfully, Hugo here begins to draw all his characters together towards the climax of the revolution. Not all will be on the same side: Javert, for instance, will be there as a police officer, and Valjean as an angel of mercy; and even among the revolutionaries motivations will differ widely. Marius will fling himself into it because he has lost the only thing in life he cares about; M. Mabeuf because he simply cannot afford to go on living; and even among the Friends of the A.B.C. the emotions are not entirely political. This only adds to the realism of the events, however, and to the credibility of their actions.

In French, a climax is known as a *noeud*, or knot, and the denouement is the untying of that knot. Hugo in the last two parts has given us an excellent example of the aptness of the term. At the beginning of Part Three, the lives of most of the characters of *Les Misérables* were single threads scattered all over Paris and its nearby villages. Thénardier with his colonel at Waterloo, Cosette and Marius, Enjolras and Gavroche, appeared to have nothing whatever to do with one another. Gradually Hugo has tied these threads together, knotting Marius and Cosette together by Eponine, Valjean and Javert by Thénardier, Gavroche and M. Gillenormand through the little lost boys. Now he throws a final loop about them, and, like the fine dramatist he is, draws them all gently toward a common center.

Book X

Summary

An insurrection is a sudden conflagration that spreads without pattern, fed by every disappointment, from disillusioned idealism to vile resentment. But for all its destructiveness it is not *ipso facto* reprehensible. Insurrections are wrong when they are an attempt of the minority to frustrate the general will. When they serve the aims of democracy they become sublime. "Insurrection," says Hugo, "is sometimes resurrection." According to this distinction, and in spite of appearances, the uprising of 1832 was legitimate. Furthermore, it gave rise to such acts of heroism that even its critics speak of it with respect.

When a situation is sufficiently combustible, it takes but a spark to light the fires of revolt. In 1832 the occasion is provided by the burial of General Lamarque, hero of the Empire and later a political leader of the left. On June 5, the funeral procession crosses Paris followed by a seditious crowd, armed and prepared for action. The dimensions of the popular unrest worries the government. It has posted 24,000 soldiers in Paris and 30,000 in the suburbs. Near Austerlitz Bridge, someone—no one knows who—fires three shots, and the storm breaks. A vast and lethal improvisation changes Paris into an armed camp. Flags are unfurled, weapons requisitioned, arms factories pillaged. In less than an hour 27 barricades go up in the Halles district alone. The center of Paris, transformed into an impregnable citadel, becomes the heart of the insurrection.

The authorities retaliate by mobilizing all their forces, including the National Guard. But the military leaders hesitate to give the order to attack. A dreadful feeling of suspense hangs over the city, for the population senses that it is not a few disgruntled acts of protest, but a large-scale uprising, that is in prospect.

Commentary

Hugo's account of the revolt of 1832 is taken from his own memories of the uprising as it appeared from the passage du Saumon, where he himself was stationed; from the experiences a friend, Jules Resseguier, recounted to him; and from a book on the revolt, *Le Cloitre Saint-Mery*, by Ray-Dusseuil. In this book there appear a real gamin and a real student who play the roles and suffer the fates of Gavroche and Enjolras in the novel, but as we have seen, Hugo has made both full-fledged characters in his book. As is natural with such sources, the whole account breathes the realism and immediacy of eyewitness testimony.

The chapters on the revolt form a counterpart to the book on Waterloo, and Hugo uses the same mingled irony and pathos, poetry and action, to arouse our emotions. Chapter 3 is an excellent example of his technique. He has already compared the coming rebellion to the natural phenomenon of a gathering storm, and he describes the progression of the revolt here in terms of the same metaphor. He describes first the "rumors" among the populace — the first faint rumblings of thunder on the horizon; then the massing, aligning, and remingling of the mob behind the cortege that, watched by the hidden eyes of fearful women and children, resemble the rapid shifting and massing of the thunderclouds; and finally the shots that, like the first lightning bolt, open the sky for the deluge. Interspersed with these images are precise and convincing details of conversation, visual impressions, and incidents, and two observations that underline the historic irony and grandeur of the moment: the Duke of Reichstadt, Napoleon's heir, is dying at the same moment the crowds are considering him as their next king; and Lafayette, hero of the American War of Independence, serves as rallying-point for this new insurrection in the cause of freedom.

Books XI-XV

Summary

Gavroche decides to go to war. Without much ado he steals an old pistol from a junk shop and swaggers down the street to the accompaniment of a song from his vast repertoire. Unfortunately, the pistol does not have a hammer. Gavroche, however, is above this or any other disappointment. If his gun is less than lethal, his monolog becomes inflammatory. If he cannot afford a piece of cake, he gets immense pleasure from tearing up billboards or insulting a bourgeois. He has a choice reply to the indignant remarks of three old crones. He hurls a stone through the windows of the barber shop whose proprietor treated his two proteges so callously. Life is a continual adventure.

Now he is about to embark on his supreme adventure. At the Saint Jean market he meets Enjolras' group and decides to join forces with them. As they march, new recruits, workers, artists, students, swell their ranks. In the Rue Lesdiguières, they enlist a most unlikely firebrand, the gentle M. Mabeuf. His mind in a trance, but his posture militant, he follows the tumultuous crowd. Near the Rue des Billettes a tall graying man joins them.

As he passes in front of his own house, Courfeyrac takes advantage of the situation to grab some money and a suitcase. On the way out, he has a few words with a young worker who is waiting for Marius. The worker follows him.

Adjoining the Halles, in a decrepit neighborhood of labyrinthine and somber streets, we find the Rue de la Chanvrerie. One end is blocked by a row of tall houses in which the ancient Corinth wine shop is located. The street would be a dead end if it were not for a narrow passage, the Rue Mondétour, which leads out of it. Inexplicably, since the food is poor, the wine atrocious, and the decor rudimentary, the Corinth has become the hangout of the Friends of the A.B.C.

On June 5, two inseparable friends, Laigle (Bossuet) and Joly, are having lunch at the Corinth. They are joined by Grantaire, who takes his nourishment in liquid form. Indifferent to the trouble brewing outside, he is earnestly trying to do justice to two bottles of wine. Alcohol proves to be a melancholy muse and he rambles on wryly about the imperfections of man and God. "I hate mankind," he avers. Books are a proliferation of trivia. Women sacrifice their virtue to greed. Brutal self-interest governs international relations. God is an unimaginative creator who must forever correct his work through revolutions, great men, and assassinations. The universe is a shabby place and everything is going wrong.

After his sweeping condemnation, Grantaire attacks his second bottle. He is about to launch into another diatribe when a nine-year-old urchin brings Laigle a cryptic message from Enjolras: "A.B.C." It is his invitation to Lamarque's funeral. But the three companions prefer wine to politics and at two in the afternoon their table is strewn with empty bottles. Grantaire especially is drinking with a vengeance. He has replaced wine with a potent mixture of brandy, stout, and absinthe. Suddenly a tumult interrupts the drunken conversation. Through the window Bossuet spots Enjolras and his armed men looking for a place to erect a barricade. He suggests the space in front of the Corinth. *In vino veritas.* The location is strategically perfect.

In a flash, the houses and streets are stripped. Soon a rampart higher than a man blocks the street. Everyone participates feverishly except Grantaire, who merely looks on and perorates incoherently. Enjolras, irritated, dismisses him with a cutting remark. But Grantaire refuses to leave, promises to sacrifice his life, and collapses in a drunken stupor. Under Enjolras, Combeferre, and Courfeyrac's energetic direction the fortifications are rapidly completed. To the original barricade has been added another one, closing one side of the Rue Mondétour.

The barricide is now manned by about 50 defenders. They are a motley aggregation, including every age, all kinds of faces, an indescribable combination of arms and costumes. Among these disparate strangers reigns a spirit of perfect fraternity. Gavroche is the life of the party. A perpetual motion machine, he is everywhere. He encourages a worker, goads a student, stings everybody. Only one shadow mars his enthusiasm: he is unhappy with his useless gun.

At dusk the barricade is finished. The men are ready, the sentinels posted, and in the deepening silence the rebels wait calmly. So remarkable is their *sang-froid* that the younger men recite love poems. Gavroche alone is preoccupied. The man from the Rue les Billettes has a disturbing familiarity. Finally, dumbfounded, the young boy finds the key to the mystery. When Enjolras approaches him to send him on a reconnaissance mission, Gavroche gives him a stunning piece of information: "Do you see the tall man?" "Well?" "He's a spy."

Enjolras immediately interrogates the suspect, who haughtily admits his double identity. His papers confirm his confession. It is Javert, and his orders are to spy on the insurrectionists. He is tied up and condemned to be shot just before the capture of the barricade. Gavroche, exultant, goes out to reconnoiter, but not before laying claim to Javert's gun: "I'm leaving you the musician, but I want the clarinet."

Revolutions, while they breed heroism, also bring out the dark side of man. Thus it happens that a certain Le Cabuc conceives the idea of posting a sniper on top of a tall building. But the fearful tenants have locked the door. Le Cabuc tries fruitlessly to break it down. Attracted by the noise, the porter sticks his head out the window. When he refuses to unlock the door, Le Cabuc shoots him. Without a moment's hesitation Enjolras grabs the killer by the shoulder and forces him to kneel, gives him a few minutes to prepare himself for death, and executes him. To a silent audience he delivers a funeral oration in which he expresses horror for his necessary act and hopes for a future where the reign of love will replace that of death.

Meanwhile Marius, overwhelmed by despair, interprets the voice that has called him to join his friends at the barricade as an order from destiny. Driven by a death wish, he makes his way through the crowd, eludes the troops, and finds himself in a no-man's land, an immense, dark vacuum. Only the agonized voice of Saint Merry's tocsin disturbs the silence.

In the total darkness Marius spots the red light of a torch and goes toward it. He reaches the Rue de la Chanvrerie barricade, but before he steps inside, he stops to examine the flux of contradictory emotions that surge in his heart. First he is proud to imitate his father's bravery; then he shudders at the ignoble nature of the conflict in which he is about to participate. But his despair, his duty to his friends, show him no alternative. Finally an illuminating thought sweeps away his hesitations. Wars are not judged by the identity of the opponents, whether they are foreigners or compatriots. All wars are internecine, since we are all brothers. Wars find their justification in their ideal. Consequently, Marius' cause is just, since he is about to fight for freedom.

At ten in the evening the long wait of the revolutionists at the barricade ends. Gavroche sings a warning and regains the barricade, out of breath after his patrol. The rebels take up their combat positions. A moment later they hear the growing sound of steady, unhurried footsteps. A disembodied voice asks: "Who goes there?" At the reply:

"French Revolution," a heavy volley shakes the barricade and knocks down the flag. One man volunteers to put it up again: Mabeuf. Like a specter he climbs the barricade, to the awe of the spectators. With a cry of "Long live the Republic!" he falls back, cut down by a bullet.

While the insurrectionists pay Mabeuf their last respects, the army attacks and manages to climb over the rampart. Gavroche and Courfeyrac are in mortal danger. In the nick of time Gavroche's assailant receives a bullet in the forehead and Courfeyrac's is hit in the chest. Marius has joined the fight in a spectacular manner. Immediately a soldier takes aim at him, and his death seems inevitable, but a young worker puts his hand on the barrel of the soldier's gun and saves Marius' life at the expense of his own.

The other insurgents are being pushed back by the army swarming over the barricade. Most of them have taken refuge inside the wine shop. A sudden thundering threat imposes a cease-fire. Marius is standing on top of the wall with a torch in his hand, ready to put it to a powder keg. "Go away," he cries, "or I'll blow up the barricade." The soldiers who are scrambling on the barricade, impressed by his earnestness, retreat in disorderly haste.

The joy of the besieged is dampened by a sobering discovery. Jean Prouvaire, one of their bravest comrades, has been made prisoner. Combeferre suggests that Jean be exchanged for Javert. The plan proves futile, however: no sooner has Combeferre stopped speaking than a vibrant voice cries, "Long live France! Long live the future!" followed by the report of a rifle. Jean Prouvaire has been executed.

While everybody's attention is engaged by the main barricade, Marius decides to inspect the small one, which is completely deserted. He is about to return to his comrades when a weak voice calls, "Monsieur Marius!" He is startled because he recognizes the voice: it is the same one which that morning had called him to the barricades. Shocked, Marius discovers Eponine crawling toward him. She has a wound in her hand, for she was the worker who deflected the bullet aimed at him. But she also has a mortal wound in her body, for she took the full impact of the shot. Marius takes her head in his lap and listens to her pathetic confession, her happiness at finding him at the supreme moment, her jealousy that made her lure him to the barricade in the hope of his death, her change of heart that saved his life at the last moment. She also tells him that she is Gavroche's sister and that she has a letter for Marius.

After Eponine dies, Marius gently kisses her on the forehead as he has promised. He enters the inn to open the letter she has given him, for he feels the impropriety of reading it beside her body. It is a note from Cosette informing him of her departure from the Rue Plumet. He is momentarily elated by this proof of love, but only momentarily, since the possibility of their marriage remains as remote as ever. He resigns himself once more to death and makes his last dispositions. He writes a note to Cosette to be delivered by Gavroche. This way he will kill two birds with one stone: assure his sweetheart of his love and save the urchin. Then he leaves instructions to have his body delivered to his grandfather.

Gavroche, afraid he will miss the great encounter, is reluctant to accept the errand. He undertakes it only because he intends to return immediately rather than wait until the next day as Marius has suggested.

On June 4, just before the insurrection, Valjean moves to his retreat in the Rue de l'Homme Armé. So deep is his alarm that he overrides Cosette's unprecedented objections. Once installed in his new quarters, he feels reassured, for the Rue de l'Homme Armé is located in an obscure and neglected neighborhood. Cosette, on the other hand, is deeply distraught. She spends the day in her room and appears only for dinner. Then, pleading a headache, she leaves the table.

Cosette's chagrin does not disturb Valjean's tranquility. He is in an optimistic mood and has radiant visions of renewed happiness in England. A heartbreaking discovery shatters his dream. On the table there is a mirror which reflects Cosette's blotter and rights its inverted message: Cosette's letter to Marius. At first, Valjean refuses to accept the evidence, but the message remains inexorably in the mirror.

Now he who has never yielded to temptation feels himself weakening, for the supreme test is the loss of one's beloved. The voice of the devil is particularly insistent, well-nigh irresistible, when love is concentrated in one person, when one single being is the object of an affection usually divided among brother, mother, and wife, and when a stranger threatens to destroy that love. Jean Valjean, in the tragic despair of old age, succumbs to hatred and goes to sit on the doorstep and contemplate the depth of his misfortune.

There Gavroche finds him, and, touched as always by the radiance of childhood, Valjean engages him in conversation. He hands him some money and indulgently allows him to break a few streetlights. Then with a little lie he persuades the urchin to hand him Marius' letter and tell him where Marius is. Gavroche disappears into the night, breaking another streetlight by way of goodbye.

Gripped by an overwhelming emotion, Valjean hurries to his room and reads Marius' words: "I am dying. When you read this my soul will be near you." His first reaction is an ugly feeling of triumph, of exultation at fate's convenient solution to his problem. But the mood quickly subsides and an hour later he makes his way to the Halles in the uniform of the National Guard.

Returning to his post, Gavroche is singing a love song with unquenchable good humor. On the way he spots a drunken man sleeping it off in a cart, and he requisitions the vehicle for the revolution. He deposits its occupant on the pavement and leaves him a receipt in the name of the Republic. Unfortunately his triumphal march is also very noisy and attracts the attention of a sergeant of the National Guard. Gavroche favors him with a few choice insults and shoves the cart into his stomach. The soldier falls, his gun goes off, and his comrades, rushing to his rescue, fire wildly in all directions for the next 15 minutes. From a safe distance, Gavroche enjoys his handiwork, then goes on his way with a disrespectful gesture and a farewell song.

Commentary

In this section, the revolt claims its first lives. The deaths of M. Mabeuf and Eponine, however, have their splendor as well as their tragedy. M. Mabeuf has deliberately committed suicide rather than endure the shameful humiliation of starving to death, and his gesture has its reward. After a lifetime in which he has vainly sought the respect and admiration of his fellow citizens by study and science, his last moments in the incongruous role of freedom fighter win him a lasting glory. As for Eponine, she too has in a sense committed suicide by turning on herself the bullet meant for Marius. For her as for M. Mabeuf, the future held nothing but shame and suffering, and her brief instants in Marius' arms are probably the only moments of real happiness she has experienced since childhood.

The deaths of Le Cabuc and the porter, however, cast a more somber light on this scene of violence. War brings out the baser as well as the nobler instincts in man, and the innocent suffer. Enjolras' prompt punishment of the criminal and his touching vision of a more perfect world temper somewhat the horror of this motiveless assassination, and the fact that he is willing to execute one of his own men also serves to underline the absolute purity and rectitude of his ideals, but Hugo never lets us forget the lolling head of the innocent corpse in the background.

In fact the scene at the barricades by night is another of the masterly tableaux in black and white that gives *Les Misérables* much of its power over our imaginations. This time, however, the light comes not from the moon but from a flaring torch that illuminates a splash of scarlet in the background. When Marius arrives he sees dimly beyond the gathered insurgents "a sort of spectator or witness who seemed to him unusually attentive. It was the porter killed by Le Cabuc. . . . A long trail of blood which had flowed from that head ran down in a scarlet network from the window to the level of the second floor, where it stopped."

Once again Jean Valjean makes one of his extraordinary decisions, expressed in actions rather than words or thoughts. But the meaning of that decision is, like his decision in Part Two to go to Arras, ambiguous until the last moment, and ambiguous perhaps even to Valjean himself.

His hatred for Marius is real, and so is his delight at the thought that the revolution may eliminate him from Cosette's life. Jean Valjean is not a milksop, and his conversion by the bishop did not, as we have seen, guarantee him the exercise of perfect and effortless goodness for the rest of his life. There is, and always has been, evil in him—as there is in any man—and if he falls prey to it, the unusual strength and cunning that have made him a remarkably good man will make him an appallingly evil one. Marius was not wrong to mistrust him after the scene in Thénardier's garret; his unusual potentialities will always make him a frightening as well as an impressive personality.

Valjean puts on his National Guard uniform and leaves the house. Why? To join the Guard and make sure Marius dies or simply to make his way safely through the streets? Hugo does not tell us, and perhaps Valjean himself does not know. But, as at M.-sur-M., if his conception of what he is about to do is not clear, his instinctive knowledge of what he is *not* about to do does not fail him.

PART FIVE: JEAN VALJEAN

Book I, Chapters 1-10

Summary

The barricade, on the Rue de la Chanvrerie, far from yielding, has been fortified. The wounded have been bandaged, lint prepared, and new bullets made. On the other hand, food has run out and the defenders are beginning to suffer from hunger. Since there is no food, Enjolras forbids the men to drink.

Dawn is coming, and the insurgents, unwilling or unable to sleep, are chatting. The conversation does not reflect their desperate position. Its tone is optimistic: humorous, literary, or philosophical. This mood, however, is shattered by Enjolras, who brings back from his reconnaissance the disastrous news that a large force has been assigned to take the barricade and that the populace as a whole has not joined the uprising. Optimism gives way to despair, but not to defeatism. The insurrectionists swear to fight to the last man.

But Enjolras refuses to accept such a sacrifice. He brings out four National Guard uniforms that he has laid aside for just such an emergency. They will provide a safe passage out for four men. No one, of course, wants to go, but Combeferre points out the uselessness of heroism and calls on the family men to leave and carry on the fight by protecting young girls from prostitution and children from hunger. In a sublime competition of generosity, each married man then pleads with the others to go. Finally five are taken out of the ranks—but there are only four uniforms. At this moment, a fifth uniform drops on top of the others. It is that of Jean Valjean, who has just entered the barricade. He is welcomed as a friend and a savior.

At this supreme moment, Enjolras is immune to fear; instead, he is carried away by a utopian vision of the future and predicts the reign of equality, justice, and liberty—the enlightenment to be brought about by education, the harmony to be born from their sacrifice. Marius does not share Enjolras' exaltation. He is still numb with grief and the world has for him the unreality of a dream. Even the arrival of Cosette's "father" makes little impression on him.

The drama of the night has driven Javert from everyone's mind. After the departure of the five married men Enjolras suddenly remembers him, gives him a glass of water, and ties him more comfortably on the table. The action attracts Valjean's attention, and he recognizes his old enemy. Javert turns his head and without surprise recognizes Valjean.

At daybreak, the attack begins with the thundering rattle of an approaching piece of artillery. A cannon appears and Enjolras yells: "Fire!" The rain of bullets misses its target and the cannon moves forward; but its first shot falls harmlessly on the pile of debris that forms the outer section of the barricade. Simultaneously with the shell, Gavroche lands in the barricade with a cheerful, "Present!" His arrival is hailed with delight by his comrades but with dismay by Marius, who had hoped to spare him this ordeal. Gavroche, however, knows no fear and with insouciant courage requests a gun.

The cannoneers rectify their aim and ricochet grapeshot off the wall. This time they are more successful: two insurgents are killed, three wounded. Enjolras carefully points his gun at the sergeant commanding the battery, squeezes the trigger, and kills him. But he feels no sense of triumph, only grief at the death of his enemy. The cannoneers, however, prepare to fire again. A mattress is needed to absorb the shots. Valjean spots one protecting a window and, with prodigious marksmanship, shoots at the ropes holding it and cuts it down. Unfortunately it falls outside the barricade. Coolly, Valjean steps out in range of enemy fire and retrieves it.

At dawn of this same day, Cosette wakes after a sweet dream of Marius. Believing he has received her letter and will soon come to see her, she rises and dresses quickly, and goes to her window to watch for Marius. Finding she cannot see the street from there, she cries for a short time, then hears the sound of cannons. Cosette does not recognize the sound and becomes absorbed in watching a family of martins nesting just below her window.

Commentary

Jean Valjean, ex-convict and wanted man, is out of place among the forces of "law and order." Arriving at the wine shop, he takes off his uniform and jumps the barricade.

Once inside, Valjean instantly belongs there. He is the right man, arrived at the right time with the right gift. And it is perfectly fitting that he, who has been one of Les Misérables and who has spent much of his life helping them privately and secretly, should at the moment of reckoning act openly on their behalf. Neither Javert nor Marius are truly among the "misérables," however, and his attitude toward both of them remains ambiguous.

The short chapter concerning Cosette is a welcome relief from the agonies and excitement of the insurrection.

Summary

The assailants of the barricade keep up their fire, hoping to provoke a riposte, exhaust the defenders, and then charge. But Enjolras does not fall into the trap. Impatient and curious, the army dispatches an observer to a roof overlooking the barricade. Valjean hits him squarely in the helmet and does the same to his successor. Bossuet asks why he did not kill him; Valjean does not answer.

Another cannon is brought up, and the attack suddenly becomes destructive. Aimed at the top of the barricade, it shatters the paving stone, and the flying fragments force the insurgents to withdraw. The wall, left undefended, is now ripe for an assault. Enjolras sees the danger and orders the artillerymen put out of commission. A well-aimed salvo kills two-thirds of them, but it is a Pyrrhic victory. Too many bullets have been wasted.

Gavroche casually decides to remedy the situation. Like a housewife doing her shopping, he grabs a basket, jumps outside the protective wall, and empties into his basket the cartridge-bags of the dead soldiers lying in the street. He is temporarily protected by a thick curtain of smoke, but his boldness leads him too close to the enemy line; the soldiers notice him and begin to shoot. Undeterred he continues his harvest; in fact he stands up straight and sings a little ditty. As the bullets rain around him, he jumps, darts, disappears, reappears, plays a frightening game with death. Finally his magic fails him, and he falls wounded. Gavroche, however, will not die without a swan song. He manages to sit up and sing another stanza of his mocking song. Then another bullet, this time fatal, cuts him down.

As Gavroche falls on his face and stops moving, two waifs are wandering hand in hand through the deserted Luxembourg Gardens. They are the two brothers whom, unknown to himself, Gavroche took under his wing. Today, June 6, 1832, the gardens are an earthly paradise, a riot of flowers, birds, and insects, bathed in sunshine. But to this festive tableau the two little boys add a somber accent, for they are hungry.

Their solitude is disturbed by a prosperous bourgeois accompanied by his six-year-old son, who is listlessly eating a brioche. The father is giving his offspring such edifying instruction as the maxim "The wise man is happy with little." When his son tires of his brioche he advises him to feed it to the swans, to teach him compassion. With laudable thrift he tries to attract their attention before the brioche sinks. Then the noise of the insurrection grows louder and the father, as prudent as he is wise, takes his son home. As soon as the pair is out of sight, the older Thénardier boy fights the swans for the soggy brioche and shares it with his brother. It is their meal, both food and drink.

Back at the barricade, Combeferre and Marius run out to retrieve the basket and carry back the child's body. Gavroche's cartridges are distributed to the men, 15 apiece. Valjean refuses his share. Paradoxically, as the situation grows more hopeless, the occupants of the barricade become calmer. They seem to ignore the imminence of death. The tranquility, however, only masks an apocalyptic mood. The barricade fighters experience the ultimate emotions, anticipate the future, sink to unplumbed depths of feeling, touch eternity.

At noon Enjolras orders paving blocks brought up to the windows of the wine shop and has axes readied to cut down the stairs and bars to barricade the door. He has, however, one last job before they retreat: to execute Javert. Valjean offers, as he puts it, "to blow his brains out." His offer is readily accepted. As the bugles sound outside he cocks his pistol. But to the last Javert retains his calm bravado and observes sarcastically: "You are no better off than I am."

As the besieged rush to the defense of the barricade, Valjean leads his prisoner outside and over the side wall, out of sight of the rest. Javert calmly invites Valjean to take his revenge, but instead the ex-convict cuts his bonds. "You are free," he tells him, and adds, "I live under the name of Fauchelevent, at No. 7, Rue de l'Homme Armé." Javert is not an easy man to surprise, but Valjean's incredible behavior stuns him. He leaves slowly, then turns around to once again invite Valjean to kill him; Valjean orders him to go away. After Javert's departure Valjean fires his gun in the air and announces that the execution has been carried out.

Meanwhile, Marius too has slowly recaptured the memory of Javert and their previous encounter. Enjolras confirms his identity, and at this precise moment he hears the pistol shot and Valjean's announcement. Marius is filled with a sensation of cold horror.

At this point Hugo breaks off to discuss, in Chapter 20, the failure of the general populace to rise in 1832. He is convinced that in the long run the natural, inevitable direction of mankind is forward, but he recognizes that this march is not steady. Sometimes a specific generation places its own happiness above the general welfare. Hugo is not severe toward this selfishness; he recognizes the individual's right to prefer his own interests to those of humanity. In general, he observes, people are resistant to the more violent forms of progress such as revolutions and insurrections. They are afraid of violence and incapable of understanding the ideals that motivate them. But self-interest, however understandable, must not and will not be man's guiding principle. Paris' rejection of the insurgents was a temporary aberration, a sickness. Mankind is basically healthy. With all its relapses, failure of nerve, intermittences, it is surely marching toward its ultimate apotheosis.

At the barricade, the government troops launch an open assault. The insurgents retaliate vigorously and once more they push back the assailants. Marius and Enjolras are the two poles of the resistance. On one side Marius exposes himself impetuously. On the other side, Enjolras, more self-controlled, fights with deadly efficiency.

For a while the military situation remains a stalemate. The rebels in their almost impregnable fortification fend off the enemy. But they cannot defeat an inexhaustible supply of troops. Gradually the successive waves of soldiers sweeping over the wall wear them down. Their weapons are gone. Many are killed, almost all are wounded. Their defense is a magnificent epic. It invites comparison with Homeric deeds or medieval heroes.

The inevitable breakthrough finally takes place. The infantry makes a breach in the middle. At last, after an eternity of heroism, a few begin to weaken. First they try to take refuge in one of the houses, and then fling themselves inside the Corinth. Enjolras, the dauntless warrior, covers their retreat and manages to bar the heavy door. Marius, however, has not been able to follow the others. He begins to faint and, as he falls, feels himself supported by a vigorous hand.

Now begins the assault of the wine shop. If possible, the defense becomes even more ferocious. Paving blocks rain from all sides. Shots are fired from the cellar and the garret. When all else fails, the rebels resort to horrible weapons, bottles of nitric acid. The battle is no longer

Homeric. It is Dantesque. When the soldiers finally manage to break into the wine shop, they find only one man standing, Enjolras. His execution is immediately ordered. Enjolras crosses his arms and serenely accepts his death. So magnificent is his courage that the enraged attackers suddenly fall silent.

The silence has an unexpected result. Grantaire, dead drunk, has slept through the most savage moments of the battle. But the unusual quiet wakes him up. With the peculiar gift of some drunkards, he is not only awake but completely lucid. He takes in the whole situation at a glance. As the firing squad prepares to shoot, he cries, "Long live the Republic!" and takes his place next to Enjolras. "Kill two birds with one stone," he suggests. Then he gently asks Enjolras: "You don't mind?" A second later, Enjolras is backed against the wall pierced by bullets and Grantaire is lying at his feet.

Meanwhile, Jean Valjean has picked up Marius as he falls and carried him off with the swiftness and agility of a tiger. Around the corner from the Corinth he finds a temporary haven, but it is unfortunately also a trap. Behind him is a wall, in front a squad of approaching soldiers. His only avenue of escape is underground. As he looks wistfully downward he suddenly notices an iron grating covering a shaft resembling a well. His bitter knowledge of escape techniques stands him in good stead and in an instant he lowers Marius to the bottom of the shaft. He finds himself in a kind of subterranean corridor. The feeling is strikingly reminiscent of his descent into the convent with Cosette. The tumult of the outside world has abruptly vanished to be replaced by a profound peace, an overwhelming silence.

Commentary

Upon the sacrifice of women and old men follows the sacrifice of children and heroes, and the tragic atmosphere deepens. Eponine and M. Mabeuf wanted to die; the Friends of the A.B.C. did not, though they accept their fate with gaiety and courage. Indeed, they had a great deal to live for: 40 years of shaping a better world; and it is just this dream of a fuller life that brings them to their deaths. Moreover, Hugo suggests, through her indifference to their dream France has lost the flower of their generation. Each of them was a young man of intelligence and ability, and in the revolution they have given proof of their ability in action as well as thought, of bravery as well as brilliance. Even Grantaire, cynic and drunkard, dies as gracefully, as courteously, and as courageously as his friends.

The death of Gavroche is an even greater tragedy, for he possessed the talents of all of them combined: courage and ingenuity, humility and joy, wit and compassion; and society had even less time to profit from his gifts. The world is poorer without him—a truth that Hugo underlines by the vignette of the two lost boys scrabbling for the swans' bread after his death.

Only Jean Valjean and Marius escape, and this is not really due to any deliberate act of will or heroism on Valjean's part. He has made no attempt to shield Marius during the battle; indeed, he seems rather to be waiting for fate to decide whether it will be Cosette's father or Cosette's lover who survives. In any event, it is Javert's unexpected presence that decides the question. As the situation evolves, it becomes apparent that it is not in Valjean's nature to kill Javert in cold blood; and if he cannot kill Javert, he has lost Cosette anyway. Marius survives, Valjean picks him up, and carries him off—not out of kindness to Marius, but because it is perhaps the last gift he will ever be able to give his child.

And yet the self-sacrifice implicit in the rescue of his rival is genuine. Physically, he could have killed the snipers on the roof, could have killed Javert, could have left Marius to die. Morally, he cannot, and this was as true when he arrived at the barricade as when he left it. The obscure forces of character in him have not changed; they have simply emerged, tough and unscathed, from the ultimate test. Jean Valjean has been a good man for so long that he cannot do evil even when he would.

Book II—
Book III, Chapters 1-9

Summary

A city has in its sewers a valuable resource, says Hugo, for it has been proved that human excrement is the richest fertilizer. Man's waste of this resource is a mad prodigality. Paris, for instance, literally throws away 25 million francs a year. Not only does it neglect a precious asset, but it contributes to its unsanitary condition by poisoning the water. To perpetuate this waste Paris has erected a spectacular structure, the sewers, a gigantic sponge, an underground city with its squares, streets, and crossroads.

Besides their physical interest, the sewers are also psychologically fascinating. Throughout history they have been the scene of many dramas; countless pursuits have taken place in them. The sewers are a mirror of human vices. The garbage they harvest bears witness to man's fallibility and speaks out against his pretensions. Broken bottles speak of drunkenness; clothes that have been worn at the Opera are rotting in the mud.

Except for a dim light filtering through openings in the sewer vault, Valjean is surrounded by blackness. Nevertheless he must plunge into this vacuum, for Marius' condition is alarming. Valjean must trust almost entirely to chance, for he has no landmark. The only clue in the sewers' layout is their slope. He knows that the sewers descend toward the Seine. He therefore chooses to proceed uphill, for he does not want to emerge near the river among the crowd.

Valjean advances like a blind man, feeling the wall with one hand and holding Marius on his back with the other. After a little while, thanks to the parsimonious light glimmering through a distant manhole, he gets a vague impression of his surroundings. While the light provides some mental comfort, it is of no practical help whatsoever. Even with the best visibility no one can find his way in this vast labyrinth, this unexplored territory. Valjean, in spite of his fortitude, cannot help contemplating with horror the perils of his situation. Will he find an exit? Will he find it in time? Will he stumble on some insurmountable obstacle? Will he die of starvation, and Marius of loss of blood?

Then he makes a disturbing observation. Instead of climbing, he is now going downhill. He wonders apprehensively whether his calculations were wrong and he is going in the direction of the Seine after all. It is too late to retrace his steps and Valjean continues to advance. Without knowing it, he has made the right decision. The sewers empty not only in the Seine but also in the outer sewer. For a half hour Valjean continues to walk without resting, trusting almost entirely to chance. The only rational decision he can make is to choose the larger corridors on the assumption that the smaller ones will lead to a dead end.

Suddenly Valjean notices his shadow in front of him, profiled against a reddish background. Dumbfounded, he turns around and sees a ball of fire in the distance. It is the lantern of a police patrol, for the authorities have readily surmised that some of the insurgents might try to escape through the sewers. Valjean, too exhausted to understand the full gravity of the situation, nevertheless flattens himself against the wall and remains motionless. The police conclude that they have heard an imaginary noise and proceed to the neighborhood of the insurrection. Just in case, they fire a parting shot, but it hits the vault above Valjean's head. Slowly darkness and silence recapture the sewers. When the patrol is safely gone Valjean resumes his march.

It must be said to the credit of the police that not even extraordinary events like an insurrection distract them from their customary enforcement of the law. Thus during June 6 in the afternoon on the right bank of the Seine near the Invalides Bridge a policeman is shadowing a thief. They are proceeding without haste, keeping an equal distance between them. But the fugitive, beneath his calm, feels the hostility and fear of a tracked animal. The policeman hails a passing cab and orders it to follow.

The chase takes the two adversaries to a ramp leading to the Champs Elysees. It seems likely that the thief is going to take the ramp, for the Champs Elysees is a wooded area tempting to a fugitive. To the surprise of the policeman, he avoids the exit and continues straight ahead. His decision is inexplicable, since the bank terminates in a dead end when the river makes a bend. When he comes to the end of the road the thief ducks behind a pile of debris. The policeman quickens his step, expecting to trap his quarry. When he too rounds the debris he discovers to his surprise that his prey has vanished. The thief has disappeared into the opening of a sewer. But this disappearance is not without an element of mystery, for to open the grating the outlaw needed a key that could only be obtained from the authorities. Though he has been outwitted, the policeman with the blind persistence of a hunting dog takes up a meaningless vigil.

In the sewer, Valjean refuses to rest, but he is encountering increasing difficulties. The ground is slippery. The low vault forces him to march bending over. Hunger and, above all, thirst torment him. In spite of his strength the inevitable exhaustion begins to take its toll. At three o'clock Valjean arrives at the outer sewer. There he is confronted by vital decisions. He has to choose among the several corridors that join at this point and he picks the wider one. Then he must decide whether to go downhill or uphill. He prefers to descend, on the assumption that the downward march will lead him to the Seine. His luck serves him well and saves his life. The other direction would have taken him to a dead end or an inextricable jungle.

Shortly after, Valjean is forced to make a halt. He deposits Marius tenderly on a bank, feels his heart beating, and bandages his wounds as best he can. Then he contemplates Marius with inexpressible hatred. After reading the note in Marius' pocket giving instructions to deliver his body to his grandfather's, and eating a piece of bread he also finds there, Valjean resumes his march with Marius on his back. Night is falling and the openings are getting rarer. The obscurity proves to be a near disaster, for it camouflages dreadful traps known as "fontis," mudholes in the ground of the corridors with all the dangers of quicksand. They hold for their victims a similar death, unexpected, lonely, inexorably slow. In addition, they have their own refinements: darkness, filth, fetidness. Sewers add degradation to the final agony.

Jean Valjean feels the pavement disappearing under his feet, plunging in a pool of water and a bed of mud. Of necessity, he goes forward and sinks with every step. Soon he is forced to throw his head back and hold up Marius' at arm's length. At last, on the verge of death, he touches solid ground and climbs out of the mire. He stumbles on a stone and falls to his knees. This position of prayer turns his thoughts toward God. In a fervent dialog he purges his heart of hate. The journey now becomes torture, for Valjean's strength has completely abandoned him. At every few steps he has to pause to catch his breath. Once he is forced to sit down and he is almost unable to get up.

Suddenly he feels a surge of energy, for in front of him he spots the beckoning light of an exit. He rushes toward it like a soul fleeing from hell. When he reaches it he has, alas, a shattering disappointment. The grating is locked. Maddened by a tantalizing glimpse of Paris and freedom, Valjean shakes the bars frantically, but it is as futile as trying to pull the teeth of a tiger. He collapses to the ground drained of hope. Valjean feels himself caught in death's web.

As darkness invades his soul, Valjean feels a hand on his shoulder and hears a whisper, "Share and share alike." He is dumbfounded to find a man in this forgotten place, even more startled to recognize Thénardier. However, he immediately regains his presence of mind and notes that Thénardier does not recognize Valjean through the mask of blood and mud. Thénardier, taking him for a murderer with his victim, proposes a characteristic deal. For half of the profit he'll open the grating. He starts a conversation by way of getting Valjean to betray himself, but Valjean maintains a stubborn silence. At last, Thénardier returns to the original subject, in terms that allow no evasion: "How much did the guy leave in his pockets?"

Valjean for once is without funds, and he can offer only 30 francs. Dissatisfied, Thénardier searches him and in passing manages to tear off a piece of Marius' jacket for later identification. He takes the 30 francs, completely forgetting the terms of the deal. He inspects the outside and silently opens the door, letting Valjean out. For a moment Valjean is overwhelmed by the majestic serenity that greets him, the reassurance of twilight, the immensity of the starry sky, the murmur of the river. Then he senses a presence behind him and recognizes Javert's ubiquitous figure.

Javert, however, is not a superman. He has been looking for Thénardier, not Valjean; at first, in fact, he does not recognize his perennial quarry. It is Valjean who identifies himself and offers no resistance to Javert's iron grip. He asks just one favor, to be allowed to take Marius home. Contrary to his behavior at M.-sur-M., Javert consents and calls his waiting cab. The trip is like the funeral procession of three cadavers.

Commentary

A book could be written about the fascination Paris sewers hold, not only for twentieth-century tourists, but for much nineteenth-century literature. Hugo, however, sums up neatly their persistent attraction for the inquiring mind: their technical ingenuity, their participation in the romance of "secret passageway," their grim summation of human existence.

Hugo skillfully weaves them into the epic pattern of his novel. They not only serve as counterpart to the passage in which he describes the "underworld mine" of criminal Paris, but provide him with a structural, picturesque, and psychological climax to a long sequence of similar scenes. Jean Valjean had fled alone in fear, carrying the beloved burden Cosette; now he flees with Marius, carrying hatred and despair on his back. He has experienced many scenes of darkness: darkness lit by a crucifix in the bishop's chamber, darkness lit by the moon with Cosette at the well, darkness lit by a flaring torch at the barricades; but now the darkness is total and absolute.

And the darkness is within his soul as well. He has saved Marius, but this has not freed his spirit. He is still drowned in hatred, and there is not a glimmer of comfort or hope upon the black path before him. Like Aeneas, like Dante, Valjean has descended into hell; but it is only a last stage on his journey into light, and as he emerges from the sewers he emerges, through prayer, from his spiritual torment also.

The deeper significance of this emergence into the light of the friendly stars is underlined by the presence of Thénardier and Javert, standing like Charon and St. Michael upon the threshold of a better life. Thénardier has always been Valjean's criminal alter ego, and even now for a moment Thénardier's evil magic seems to work again, making us wonder whether Valjean has not after all really killed Marius. But in the face of this new Valjean, Thénardier's influence ebbs, and he meekly opens the door to freedom. Javert the avenging angel is a more implacable doorkeeper, but judgment must always precede paradise on Resurrection Day.

Book III, Chapters 10-12 —
Book IV

Summary

Night has fallen when the cab reaches its destination. The house is asleep. Javert knocks and has Marius' body, as he imagines it to be, transported upstairs. While M. Gillenormand's servants go for the doctor and prepare bandages, Javert leaves unobtrusively, accompanied by Valjean. In the cab, Valjean risks one more request. He asks for permission to see Cosette. This request, too, is quietly granted.

When they arrive at the Rue de l'Homme Armé, Javert dismisses the cab. The procedure is a little unusual, but Valjean assumes that he is to be taken on foot to the police station. Unusual too is Javert's discretion in allowing his prisoner to see Cosette alone. On the landing Valjean, weakening at the prospect of a heart-wrenching tête-à-tête, stops for a minute and distractedly looks out of the window. The lamplight reveals a deserted street.

At M. Gillenormand's, a camp bed is set up for Marius at the doctor's orders. A careful examination reveals no fatal wound. Marius is not out of danger, however. His loss of blood has exhausted him, his collarbone is fractured, his head has been injured by sword cuts, and he may have a skull fracture. The doctor, feverishly working to stop the bleeding, looks pessimistic.

In spite of all efforts to keep the news from him, M. Gillenormand is awakened by the commotion and appears, ghost-like in his white nightgown. When he sees his grandson, apparently dead, he is overcome by an immense grief which quickly rises to a paroxysm of despair. In his hysteria he accuses Marius of having got himself killed in revenge. Then he turns his wrath on the liberals and babbles reminiscences of Marius' golden childhood, followed by murmured laments on Marius' wasted life and his own lonely old age. At this moment, Marius slowly opens his eyes and M. Gillenormand faints.

Javert slowly walks away from Valjean's house. For the first time in his life he is in the throes of indecision. As he meditates painfully, he reaches the Seine and leans on the parapet, absentmindedly contemplating its swirling waters. To arrest Jean Valjean is personal ingratitude, but to let him go is an inconceivable breach of duty. A more introspective man might be able to solve the dilemma. But Javert, a mental automaton governed by rigid principles, has always avoided thinking. Now, however, a new, unprecedented, unacceptable idea is forcing its way into his consciousness. There is a higher law than the judicial apparatus. A man can be an outlaw and still be virtuous. Valjean must be respected, not only for his latest act of generosity, but for all the good he did as M. Madeleine. Javert is entering a new moral universe; his narrow, uncomplicated world is crumbling. He is "an owl forced to gaze with the eye of an eagle."

But Javert's myopia is incurable. He cannot reject the values of a lifetime and survive. He cannot reconcile himself to his own act. For him, the freeing of Valjean is a clear violation of the law, hence inexcusable. Incapable of executing what he considers his duty, Javert must find some other way of making peace with his intransigent conscience. At last he sees a way. Firmly he enters a nearby police station, takes some writing material, and addresses to the prefect various recommendations for the improvement of the police administration. Then he returns to his previous position at the Seine parapet. The night is pitch black. The streets are deserted. The river is invisible and only betrays itself by the sound of its rushing whirlpools. Javert contemplates for an instant the precipice, takes off his hat, climbs the parapet, and disappears into the gaping obscurity.

Commentary

Thénardier has given Valjean his physical freedom; Javert completes the task by giving him his legal freedom. Spiritually, Valjean has already freed himself and is now truly M. Leblanc: the "white" man, the man with no name, who belongs only to God. A single force has brought him out of the slough of ignorance and evil: the power of love. Love, first, for the bishop; then love of Cosette; and finally, as he shows on the barricades, love of mankind.

In contrast, Javert has always feared and mistrusted love. It twists things, changes things: it is not "in order." Lost, lonely bloodhound that he is, he feels safe only with what is tangible, organized, immutable; if he loves anything, it is the law that has always kept a warm place in a corner for him and told him exactly what to do next. Now, in a revelation like that on the road to Emmaus, he discovers that the law is not enough, that there is a more powerful force to which even the law must bow and which can make even him, Javert, go against his conscience. He sees the light of love, but it is too shattering for him to endure.

"Justice," of which Javert is a personification, says critic Georges Piroué, "cannot accept into its corpus the foreign body of contradiction;" only the divine justice based on charity can do this, and in fact constantly renews itself by so doing. The reign of justice must be destroyed before the reign of charity can begin, and Javert must die so that Jean Valjean may live. His death, however, is not so much a defeat as a transformation. By loving Javert, Valjean has destroyed him, but he has saved him too; and divine justice will reward Javert's crime against human justice.

Books V-VI

Summary

Marius' recovery is long and difficult. Suffering from a concussion, racked by delirium, covered with infected wounds, he remains at death's door for several weeks. As long as he is in danger, M. Gillenormand does not leave his bedside. Another man, a white-haired gentleman, also takes an interest in the convalescent. He comes daily to inquire about the state of his health.

It takes Marius six months to recover. The lapse of time has cooled all political passion and Marius receives a *de facto* amnesty. His gradual recovery fills his grandfather with ecstasy. M. Gillenormand celebrates his cure by giving his servant three louis, singing a licentious eighteenth-century song, and even, according to an eyewitness, praying.

Marius himself is not so happy. He is still obsessed by the thought of Cosette, and he has resolved not to accept the gift of life without love.

He is determined to marry Cosette even if it means defying his grandfather. And he is convinced that all M. Gillenormand's new affection is still conditional on Marius' compliance with his wishes. Finally, angrily, he announces his plans to marry. M. Gillenormand, incredible though it seems to Marius, is enchanted and expresses the greatest enthusiasm for Cosette. Their interview ends with a complete emotional reconciliation, and Marius even calls M. Gillenormand by the magic name of "Father." The old man arranges for an immediate visit from Cosette and even painfully suppresses a diatribe against the Revolution.

Cosette appears in a state of happy bewilderment, ecstatic, blushing, shy before so many bystanders. Fauchelevent-Valjean, dressed with sober correctness, stands quietly to one side with a smile that expresses more poignancy than joy. M. Gillenormand greets him courteously but mispronounces his name with aristocratic negligence. Overcome by emotion, Marius is unable to speak, but Cosette in an uninterrupted monolog pours out her anxiety, her love, her joy.

M. Gillenormand seems happiest of all. He hovers over the couple, marvels at Cosette's beauty, and courts her charmingly. Valjean, until now so quiet he has been forgotten, now intervenes. Without any theatrics he announces that Cosette is rich. He has at her disposal almost 600,000 francs, which he lays down on the table. M. Gillenormand is thunderstruck, but Cosette and Marius are too much in love to pay any attention to such a trivial detail.

The marriage is set for February. The two old men, each in his fashion, work for the happiness of the young couple, Valjean quietly takes care of all practical details and solves a problem Cosette is not even aware of. To spare her the stigma of illegitimacy, he passes her off as Euphrasie, the daughter of the real Fauchelevent.

Gillenormand's services, while not as valuable, are more dramatic. He raids the family heirlooms to offer the girl a shimmering collection of bibelots and jewels. He is as earnest about his frivolities as other men are about more serious matters, for to Gillenormand luxury is not merely a way of life, it is a philosophy. It is only through frills and superfluities, he says in effect, that life becomes a banquet. He waxes particularly eloquent about weddings. He contrasts the dull ceremony of the nineteenth century with the elegance, the sauciness, and the revelry of the eighteenth. His description of a wedding is a canvas inspired by Fragonard, Watteau, and Boucher.

Cosette is to be installed in the handsomest room in the house, which, moreover, is to be luxuriously redecorated. Mlle. Gillenormand, who had nothing but contempt for the young couple when she thought they would be poor, now plans to leave them all her money. Cosette comes to visit Marius daily with Valjean as chaperon. Marius tolerates him as Cosette's father but avoids any intimacy. They discuss only such neutral subjects as politics and education. Marius remembers still that when he last saw Valjean the old man was about to shoot a policeman, but as Valjean never refers to the events of the insurrection Marius cannot accuse him openly.

Marius is also preoccupied by the problem of Thénardier. Despite the man's viciousness, Marius still feels an obligation to carry out his father's last wishes. His investigation, however, fails to unearth Thénardier: all the man's associates have either disappeared or died; Thénardier himself has been condemned to death and has dropped out of sight.

Marius feels that he also owes a debt of gratitude to the unknown stranger who saved him and brought him home, but he too cannot be found. Neither the cabdriver nor the police can provide any information about him. Marius is bedeviled by a series of puzzles: why did a total stranger save his life? Why didn't the policeman in the cab arrest him? Why has his savior not appeared to claim a reward, or at least an expression of thanks? Throughout Marius' stubborn search Valjean keeps silent. Even when he hears Marius' awed reconstruction of what the escape through the sewers must have cost his rescuer, he does not utter a word.

The wedding, while it is not the mad extravaganza M. Gillenormand has dreamed of, is nevertheless a heartwarming and happy event. Only one incident mars it: Valjean has had a slight accident a few days before and, with his arm in a sling, is unable to sign any of the wedding documents. The "accident" is fortunate, since Valjean's signature as Fauchelevent would be illegal.

On the way to church the nuptial procession has to take a street filled with carriages and Mardi Gras maskers. At one point a traffic jam causes a halt, and a carriage overflowing with revelers also stops in the other line of traffic. They are a ragged, disreputable lot, noisy and sarcastic. In the midst of the general hilarity two of the maskers, an old Spaniard with an enormous nose and gigantic mustache, and a thin young girl, carefully observe the wedding party. The man is particularly interested in the father of the bride, whom he seems to recognize. He is consumed by curiosity and urges his indifferent companion, Azelma, to find out more about them.

With their marriage vows, Marius and Cosette are transfigured. They accomplish that miracle, the realization of a dream, and all the bitterness they have endured only enhances their present happiness. Back at Gillenormand's, the wedding banquet is gay. Flowers fill the house, the dining room is ablaze with lights, crystal, and precious metal. Three violins and a flute play Haydn quartets.

Valjean slips quietly away, but nothing can dim the happiness surging in the room. M. Gillenormand, champagne glass in hand, delivers an epicurean sermon, praises love, preaches joy, and enthusiastically acknowledges the eternal domination of woman. He makes of marriage the ultimate form of piety. Led by the grandfather's contagious exhilaration, the wedding feast reaches a crescendo of gaiety. At midnight the newlyweds take their leave and the houses lapses into silence.

When he leaves the party, Valjean pauses outside for a moment to listen to the muted gaiety of the banquet. Then he returns home along the same route by which he has escorted Cosette to see Marius during the past three months. In the apartment he wanders from one empty room to another, attentive to the heightened sound of his footsteps. Then he goes to his bedroom and removes the perfectly sound arm from its sling. His eyes fall on the suitcase containing the clothes Cosette wore when she left Montfermeil. Slowly he pulls them out and spreads them on the bed. Memories of his first meeting with Cosette throng to his mind, and he buries his head on the bed and sobs heartbreakingly.

All his life Valjean has waged with his conscience Jacob's fight with the angel. In spite of the ferocity of the struggle, his conscience has always won. But tonight he faces the supreme challenge. He must decide whether to impose his presence on Cosette and Marius, whether to associate his dark and illegal existence with the luminous young couple. Valjean cannot accept the renunciation that his heroic lucidity dictates. Cosette is his life raft and he cannot yet resign himself to drowning. Isn't there a limit to man's sacrifice, he wonders? Can God demand absolute annihilation? As on a previous occasion with the Champmathieu affair, Valjean contemplates his fateful alternatives through the long night.

Commentary

One by one, Hugo untangles his complications and brings them to a tidy conclusion. Jean Valjean is safe, Marius is healthy, M. Gillenormand and his grandson become completely reconciled, Cosette and Marius are united. Only one problem remains: the antipathy between Jean Valjean and Marius. And it is a genuine problem. Marius is young and callow, and fails to appreciate Valjean at his real value, it is true; but he also has extremely good reasons to mistrust him. It is hard to feel comfortable with your father-in-law when you have met him in a den of thieves and heard him shoot a policeman.

Valjean is fully aware of this problem, but he cannot help Marius. To reveal that he is the young man's rescuer would be to burden him with an uncomfortable debt of gratitude; and the explanations it would entail would saddle Cosette, too, with the details of a dark past from which he has done his best to shield her. The only solution is for him to vanish, but he cannot bring himself to do it. His struggle, however, is qualitatively unlike any he has undergone before. At Arras, at the barricades, the good in him struggled with the evil; now he undergoes a conflict between two goods, his human love for Cosette and the spiritual nobler love that demands he surrender his earthly joys for her ultimate salvation and his own. Neither choice can be a wrong one.

Books VII-IX

Summary

Late the next morning Valjean returns to the Rue des Filles du Calvaire and asks for Marius. His somber and weary air makes a strange contrast with the festive appearance of the living room. Marius greets him with the greatest cordiality. He seems to insist on disregarding the strain that has existed between them and invites Valjean to make his home with him. Valjean interrupts by blurting out that he is an ex-convict. As corroboration, he shows him his perfectly sound hand and explains the subterfuge as a means of avoiding the signing of legal documents. Appalled, Marius urges him to continue, and Valjean complies by briefly stating his background, his meeting with Cosette, and his love for her—the depth of which he does not reveal, however. His confession ends with a reference to the 600,000 francs, which he explains as a trust.

Marius is puzzled by this unnecessary honesty. Valjean answers by explaining the tyranny of his confession, which demands nothing less than absolute truth, which rejects the most compelling excuse. He cannot bear to be befriended under false pretenses. Poignantly, he refers to the tragic destiny that requires him to be despised by others in order that he may respect himself. Marius is crushed by Valjean's revelations, but is magnanimous enough to shake his hand.

The painful conversation is interrupted by Cosette's charming intrusion. She gossips, coaxes her father to smile, pleads for permission to remain. When Marius asks her to leave them in privacy, she goes, with playful reproaches and threats. Cosette's visit reminds Valjean of the emotional impact his confession will have on her, and, his face bathed in tears, he longs for death. Marius instantly promises to keep it a secret from her and offers him a reward for managing Cosette's money so scrupulously. His magnanimity, however, is mixed with aversion and he suggests that Valjean stop seeing Cosette. At first Valjean agrees, but then blanches at the magnitude of the sacrifice. He who in the past has asked nothing for himself now humbly pleads with Marius not to separate him permanently from her. He invokes his immense love, promises to come rarely and remain unobtrusive. Marius understands this pathetic plea and reluctantly allows Valjean a nightly visit.

When Valjean goes, Marius is the prey of mixed emotions, but dismay is dominant. He wonders whether he has been too lenient with Valjean, whether he should have investigated the old man more carefully. Apprehensively, he wonders if he has not paid too dearly for his happiness, if his whole life is to be tarnished by this infernal shadow. He has, certainly, a measure of esteem for his father in law. His scrupulous administration of Cosette's fortune has been admirable. His confession, so painful and so dangerous for himself, indicates a certain nobility of spirit. But Marius cannot forget the Thénardier incident nor Valjean's revenge on Javert at the barricades.

Beyond the practical considerations, Valjean poses a metaphysical problem for Marius. How can Cosette have achieved such innocence in daily contact with such evil; how could such an impure tool have created a work of such purity? God's methods are unfathomable. Ultimately, Marius' lasting impression is one of revulsion, and relief that Valjean is willing to retire into the background. In spite of his enlightenment, Marius still retains the prejudices of his time in regard to criminal matters. He does not yet understand the cruelty, even the immorality, of the French penal system, which for a single crime brands a man for life.

The next evening at dusk Valjean is respectfully greeted by a servant and introduced into a neglected, dank room on the ground floor. Two armchairs have been installed with a worn bedside rug by way of carpet. Cosette enters and greets him with the most tender affection. But Valjean remains stubbornly reserved. He refuses to kiss her, refuses her invitation to dinner, even addresses her formally as "Madame." Cosette is puzzled and disturbed by Valjean's eccentricity, especially his insistence that he be called Monsieur Jean. She pleads with him to return to their former intimacy and scolds him affectionately. Briefly Valjean yields to the poignant temptation to call Cosette "tu" ("thou," the familiar form of address), but he regains his self-control and departs with a respectful "Madame."

Cosette resigns herself to Valjean's bizarre ways. She has the room cleaned up, but otherwise accepts their painful estrangement. The rest of the household simply dismisses Valjean as an eccentric. No one suspects the agony he is suffering.

In the next few weeks Cosette's new life, new social engagements, her absorption with Marius, make the loosening of old ties easier for her. For Valjean, however, love will not die. He cannot resist the temptation to lengthen his visits. Cosette's accidental return to the word "father" brings him to the brink of tears. But the gulf between them continues to widen. Every gesture of familiarity is gradually dropped. Valjean's happiness is reduced to an hour a day of contemplation or reminiscence.

One day in April, moved by the rebirth of nature, Marius and Cosette go back on a little pilgrimage to the garden of the Rue Plumet and forget all about Valjean. Valjean is not discouraged by this involuntary snub. To prolong his visit, he even resorts to the stratagem of praising Marius. Cosette, delighted to talk about her husband, does not notice the passage of time. But Marius subtly manages to shunt Valjean aside. When the old man's visits last too long, a servant is sent to remind Cosette that it is time for dinner. At the end of April the fire is not lit in the fireplace. When Cosette orders the fire relit, the chairs are moved to a far corner.

One evening Cosette reports that Marius has asked her whether she could live on his income alone. Valjean concludes, to his great distress, that Marius suspects Cosette's money really comes from him and that it is tainted. At last Marius makes his hostility brutally clear. He has the chairs taken away, and Valjean, unable to delude himself any longer, stops coming. Cosette in her new marital happiness scarcely notices his absence. However, she does send her maid to inquire, and

Valjean generously pretends that he has been busy and is about to take a trip.

During the last months of spring and the first months of summer, 1833, Valjean takes a daily walk in the direction of the Rue des Filles du Calvaire. He is in a complete trance. When he approaches his destination he slows down, and when he reaches the street he stops. He stares ahead yearningly at his forbidden paradise and a tear slips down his cheek. Gradually, like a pendulum whose oscillations grow shorter, he abbreviates his walks.

Hugo points out that Marius feels it a matter of husbandly duty to separate Valjean from Cosette; new and mysterious information has confirmed his darkest suspicions of the old man. Cosette is almost equally blameless. Marius exerts a magnetic influence on her and almost involuntarily she yields to his wishes. In any case, her neglect of her father is only superficial; under the surface her love is as deep as ever. She does occasionally inquire about Valjean, but he encourages the estrangement by pretending to be out of town. Besides, what is known as the ingratitude of children is merely the fulfillment of the scheme of nature. It forces the young to look to life and to neglect the generation that represents the past and is journeying toward the grave.

The pendulum finally comes to a halt. One day, Jean Valjean merely takes a few steps, sits down on a milestone and returns home. The next day he does not leave his room. The following day he does not get out of bed. His janitress, who prepares his meager meal, finds the dish untouched. A week elapses and Valjean does not leave his bed. The janitress' husband, when he hears the news, pronounces the case hopeless, and the doctor, after his visit, conforms his diagnosis. He announces that Valjean is suffering from the loss of a loved one.

One evening Valjean has trouble finding his pulse. Driven by a supreme compulsion, he puts on his clothes with extreme difficulty, takes out his valise and spreads Cosette's clothes on the bed. Then he lights the bishop's candlesticks. The effect is disturbingly funereal. Every movement drains his strength. He catches a glimpse of himself in the mirror and finds he has aged 30 years. At last, after a tremendous effort, he manages to sit down and in a trembling hand writes Cosette a last letter. It contains a reassuring explanation of the source of his fortune. Suddenly he is overcome by an immense despair, by an overwhelming yearning to die in Cosette's presence. At that moment he hears a knock on the door.

One evening, as Marius has been working in his study, he has received a letter that promises important revelations about an individual living with Marius; the tobacco odor and handwriting immediately remind him of Thénardier. Happy to be able to settle his debt at last, Marius orders Thénardier sent in; but he can scarcely recognize him, for Thénardier is thoroughly disguised. Upon Marius' curt invitation to speak, Thénardier explains he wants to retire to an isolated village in Panama, but he needs money. If Marius will provide it, he will provide Marius with a secret. He tells Marius, to whet his appetite, that his father-in-law is a thief, a murderer, and an ex-convict named Jean Valjean.

Contemptuously, Marius tells him he knows that already and further demoralizes Thénardier by revealing all he knows about the former innkeeper's own background. Giving Thénardier a 500-franc bill to settle his debt of gratitude, he goes on to say that he believes Valjean had M. Madeleine arrested, stole his money, and killed Javert. Thénardier, better informed on this point than Marius, regains lost ground by triumphantly announcing that Valjean and Madeleine are the same person. With a flourish he pulls out two newspapers which confirm his allegations.

Belatedly, it begins to dawn on Marius that he has misjudged Valjean, but Thénardier insists he is, nevertheless, a thief and a murderer. To prove it, he recounts his own version of the adventure in the sewer. According to him, Valjean was there to dispose of the body of a young man whom he had murdered for his money. There he met a fugitive who provided him with a key to get out, but not before the fugitive had torn off a piece of clothing from the murdered man; and Thénardier, to clinch his case, produces a piece of black rag. Marius, dazzled by the revelation of the magnificent truth, reaches blindly into the closet and throws a black suit at Thénardier's feet. Proclaiming that he is the supposed victim, he fits the torn piece of cloth neatly into the rent in his suit. Accusingly, he turns on Thénardier and catalogs all the sins of his past life, but offers him 4,500 francs now and 20,000 the next day if he will leave and never return. Thénardier accepts and departs — to become a slave trader in America, Hugo tells us.

In feverish haste, Marius takes Cosette and speeds with her in a cab to Valjean's home. On the way, he reveals the whole story of her father's life to Cosette and comments rapturously on its ineffable saintliness. The young couple arrive in time: Valjean still lives. Choked with emotion, Cosette rushes toward him and embraces him; Marius calls him "father." Valjean is incoherent with joy. To Cosette, tenderly nestled on his lap, he pours out his immense love and poignant longing. Cosette responds with affectionate reproaches and Marius with profound gratitude and admiration. Firmly but respectfully, he declares they have come to take Valjean home with them, and Cosette paints a radiant picture of their future life together.

Valjean listens as if to a magnificent symphony, and a tear comes to his eyes. Then, sorrowfully, he announces he is dying. Cosette and Marius, heartbroken, refuse to accept the truth. Valjean, however, in the spirit of abnegation that has characterized his whole life, exhorts them to accept the wisdom of God's decision and urges them to look forward to their future happiness.

The doctor arrives and confirms the verdict. Valjean settles his earthly and spiritual affairs and, with an unexpected renewal of strength, walks to the wall, takes down the crucifix, and sits down again. He reassures Marius as to the legitimacy of his wealth, and requests an anonymous tombstone; and his last moments are filled with happy memories. He evokes Cosette's childhood, their humble pleasures, their adventures. He tells Cosette about her mother, and asks her to forgive the Thénardiers. In the presence of the two people he loves, he dies happy.

In the Père-Lachaise cemetery there is a neglected and anonymous tombstone. Time, vegetation, and the elements are slowly destroying it. Only an unusual epitaph in pencil gave it a transitory distinction.

> He sleeps. Although fate was very strange to him,
> He lived. He died when he lost his angel;
> It happened simply, as naturally as
> The night falls when the day goes away.

Commentary

Characteristically, Jean Valjean decides to speak the bitter truth about himself and conceal the sweet. Although he considers this being honest with Marius, it is not really honesty; but he has no choice. An ex-convict cannot say "I am a good man" and be believed; he has lost his credibility.

His confession clears the air temporarily, but it does not really solve anything. Some readers feel that the continuing struggle over Cosette is unworthy of Jean Valjean, that a proper hero ought simply to have gone away; but to think so is to misunderstand Jean Valjean and Hugo's vision of him. In the first place, as Hugo has been saying all along, to do right is never easy; and in the second place, when Valjean thinks of disappearing, it is not going away he has in mind; it is death. Cosette is the only thing he loves in this world, and if he gives her up he will die. And Jean Valjean, as we have seen, has a very powerful instinct for survival. He remains to the last no incredible saint, but a thoroughly human figure.

His final renunciation is a defeat, but thanks to Thénardier, it is also a victory. Through the maze of lies this man has woven about himself and everyone who comes in contact with him, the truth accidentally emerges — as it always does if a lie goes on long enough. Thénardier, evil though he is, must eventually also contribute to the apotheosis of the good; this is the law of life as God has planned it.

And so Jean Valjean, having sacrificed his last happiness, has it returned to him a hundredfold; the lonely man, the outcast, dies surrounded by the happiness he has created, and the solitary celibate has been the progenitor, through Marius and Cosette's children, of a fruitful and contented posterity. No man can ask for a happier ending.

One knot, however, Hugo has left without untangling: no one has adopted the two little lost boys Gavroche left unprotected. An oversight, perhaps; or perhaps it was intentional. Perhaps he wanted his readers to remember, every night as they tumbled into bed, that somewhere out in the cold and darkness there were still two little lost boys, and many more like them, hungry and unprotected. And that, his unspoken conclusion seems to say, is *your* business.

REVIEW QUESTIONS AND ESSAY TOPICS

1. *Les Misérables* is one of the most widely read novels of all time. How do you explain its appeal?

2. Trace Victor Hugo's numerous antitheses.

3. Comment on Hugo's preface: "As long as there shall exist, by virtue of law and custom, a social damnation artifically creating hells in

the midst of civilization and complicating divine destiny with a human fatality . . . books like this cannot be useless."

4. "My belief is that this book will be one of my major achievements, if not my major achievement." Do you agree with Victor Hugo's appraisal of his own work?

5. To those who accuse Victor Hugo of implausibility Baudelaire answers: "It is a novel constructed like a poem, where each character is an exception only by the hyperbolic way he represents a generality." Elaborate.

6. One of Victor Hugo's most poignant and recurrent themes is what François Mauriac calls "the desert of love," that is, unfulfilled love. Trace Hugo's variations on this theme.

7. One of Hugo's editors Marius-François Guyard, claims to see a solid framework behind the apparent disorder of *Les Misérables*. What is your estimate of the novel's structure?

8. To what extent is Javert a symbol and to what extent an individualized characterization?

9. Thénardier is an absolutely evil man. Can such a character be considered realistic? Is he convincing?

10. Diderot defines one form of genius as the tendency to see abstract ideas only through their concrete manifestations. How does Victor Hugo illustrate this definition in *Les Misérables?*

11. Discuss *Les Misérables* as a realistic novel.

12. It has been said that Jean Valjean's dominant emotion is *caritas* (charity — active, outgoing love for others), but that it is not his only passion. Discuss some other emotions that Jean Valjean experiences in the course of the book and show how they conflict with or reinforce his *caritas*.

13. What are the principal social evils Victor Hugo is attacking in *Les Misérables?*

14. What social reforms does Victor Hugo advocate, directly or indirectly, in *Les Misérables?*

15. What is Hugo's view of human nature? Does he believe it is naturally good or vitiated by original sin, or does he take a position somewhere between these two extremes?

16. Marius has been described as a typical young Romantic of his era. Discuss him and compare him with other Romantic heroes in books, plays, or poems of the Romantic period which you may have read.

17. Explain Cosette's function in the novel in regard to character development, plot development, and theme.

18. What are Hugo's principal weapons as a propagandist? Discuss the effectiveness of each.

19. Gavroche is considered one of the most memorable characters in French literature. Analyze the techniques Hugo has used to make him so.

20. Discuss the Romantic elements in *Les Misérables*.

SELECTED BIBLIOGRAPHY

GRANT, ELLIOTT M. *The Career of Victor Hugo*. Cambridge, Mass.: Harvard University Press, 1945.

GUIER, FOSTER. *The Titan Victor Hugo*. New York and San Francisco: Vanni, 1955.

HUGO, VICTOR. *Le Post-scriptum de ma vie*. Translated with a study of the last phase of Hugo's genius by LORENZO O'ROURKE. New York and London: Funk & Wagnalls, 1907.

JOSEPHSON, MATTHEW. *A Realistic Biography of the Great Romantic*. Garden City, N.Y.: Doubleday, Doran, 1942.

MAUROIS, ANDRE. *Olympio: The Life of Victor Hugo*. Translated by GERARD HOPKINS. New York: Harper, 1956.

MOORE, O. H. "Realism in Les Misérables," *PMLA*, LXI (March, 1946), 211-28.

heir of maternal great-aunt

Luke Esprit = 1st wife
Gillenormand

Mlle. Gillenormand (prude)

2nd wife (invests his money) = Luke Esprit Gillenormand

youngest daughter (10 yrs younger than sister)

Magnon ≠ Luke Esprit Gillenormand
(servant)

son   son

priest (rector of Academy of Poitiers)

Col. Baron Georges Pontmercy (Legion of Honor) (dies of brain fever) = 2nd wife

Baron Marius Pontmercy

Jeanne Mathieu = Jean Valjean (or Vlajean) (Brie peasant) (killed by a falling tree)
(dies of milk fever)

Jean Valjean (pruner) (Father Madeleine) [Mayor of M— sur M—] [1795] (#24,601) (Jean-the-Jack) (Urbain Fabre) (Ultimus Fauchelevent) (#9430) (M. Leblanc)

Mère Jeanne (widow)

7 children

Félix Tholomyès ≠ Fantine (Madeleine's employee) ≠ musician

Cosette (Euphrasie Fauchelevent) (the Lark) (born, 1815) (Mlle. Lenoire) (Baroness Pontmercy) = Baron Marius Pontmercy

Les Misérables Genealogy

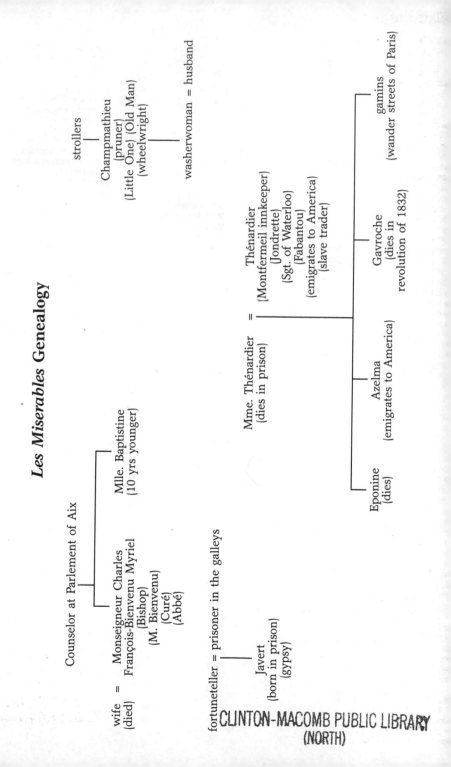